*A LITTLE
GRIEF BREAK*

The Collected Poems of Derrick C. Brown, 1995-2025

Write Bloody Publishing

writebloody.com

Copyright © Derrick C. Brown, 2025

All rights reserved. No part of this book may be used, performed, or reproduced in any manner whatsoever without written permission from the publisher except in the case of brief quotations embodied in critical articles or reviews.

First edition.
ISBN: 978-1-949342-88-8

Cover Design by Derrick C. Brown, www.brownpoetry.com
Interior Layout by Derrick C. Brown, Nikki Steele
Edited by Sam Preminger, Brooklyn Geyer, Haley Hutchinson, Melanie Robinson, and Vandie
Proofread by Wess Mongo Jolley
Author Photo by Matt Wignall

Type set in Bergamo.

Printed in the USA

Write Bloody Publishing
Los Angeles, CA

Support Independent Presses
writebloody.com

For the couches many of you have given me.

And this strange, good life.

A LITTLE GRIEF BREAK

I.
NIGHT COLLAPSER

MEET ME AT PALACE LAKE 19
ODE TO THE PUBLIC PARK 21
SHE COLLAPSED THE NIGHT 22
SUPERBLOOM 24
WATER THE POISON 27
YOU CAN SUE THE HORIZON 30
WEDDING POEM 15 33
I DON'T KNOW HOW TO SAY MY INSIDES 35
FULL METAL NECKLACES 37
SLOW THE BURN 39
READ THIS TO THE OLD MAN 41
MY JOB IS MAKING SENSE 43
TWEEN SPIRIT 44
A GLASS PAGEANT 45
COLOSSUS OF NEVER 47
BOMB THREAT CHECKLIST 2 48
HOUSE OF NEW LANGUAGE 51

II.
BORN IN THE YEAR OF THE BUTTERFLY KNIFE

THE KUROSAWA CHAMPAGNE 55
HOT FOR SORROW 57
AQUANAUT 59
WHY AMELIA EARHART WANTED TO VANISH 61
12:55 63
JOIN THE AIRBORNE 65
TOMB 67
A FINGER, TWO DOTS, THEN ME 68
CURSING JEFF BUCKLEY 72
PUSSYCAT INTERSTELLAR NAKED HOTROD MOFO! 73
CHEAP RENT... 75
LAST NIGHT IN PARIS... 77
AMAZING JIM 80

III.
I LOVE YOU IS BACK

ALL DISTORTION, ALL THE TIME 85
MY FIRST CPR CLASS 87
RECORDING TEXTBOOKS FOR THE BLIND 89
DEBBIE 91
LISTING MY CONFLICTS 92
WOMAN SLEEPING IN A ROOM OF HUMMINGBIRDS 93
THE PROFESSIONAL DRINKERS OF CALGARY, CANADA .. 95
THE VICTORY EXPLOSIONS 96
LUCKY IN LOS FELIZ 99
MY SPEECH TO THE GRADUATING CLASS 101
THE DEMONS' FIRST DATE 104
HOW THE JELLYFISH WISHES 106
SECRET POEM
IN DEFENSE OF SLEEP CONTROL 108

IV.
SCANDALABRA

COTTON IN THE AIR 113
VAGUE SUBJECT MATTER 115
VALENTINE'S DAY IN DRESDEN 116
MEATLOAF 118
CHURCH OF THE BROKEN AXE HANDLE 120
PATIENCE 124
GROCERY LIST 128
FULL METAL NECKLACES 3 126
TOP 127
THE LONG, OUTSTANDING SALTATION 130

V.

OUR POISON HORSE

THE STARGAZER IS DYING 143
THE RUINED LIFE 144
300 BONES 146
PLACES YOU SHOULD NEVER KISS 150
TONGUE ON THE WALL 151
GIRL PIZZA AT BACKSPACE IN AUSTIN 153
SOUR MASH 154
MENDER/DESTROYER 158
FAVORITE ROLLER DERBY NAMES 159
CAKE WEEK 160
TOODLE LOO 161
MULE BREAKER 162
OUR POISON HORSE 163

VI.
STRANGE LIGHT

LOVERS FIZZ 169
RINGLETS 170
OUR LONG LOW NIGHTS 171
THE BEST or MANIAC SOUL PLUMBER 173
WHEN NURSES COUGH 174
STRAY LIGHTNING 175
INSTEAD OF KILLING YOURSELF 176
NO WALLS, NO GO 177
JOY IN PLACES WITHOUT YOU 179
STRANGE LIGHT 181
DERRICK BROWN'S FAMOUS LAST WORDS 194

VII.
UH OH

EVERY COFFIN IS A SOAP BOX DERBY 199
ETHERNET BALLAD..201
STROKER OF SORROW 203
BLIZZARD 205

VIII.
HELLO. IT DOESN'T MATTER.

FIRST SKINNY DIP 209
YOU WERE ONCE THE SIZE OF A THUMB..........................211
NIGHTSTAND MUSIC 212
LITTLE BONES..213
DEEP COVER...214
THE AWFUL SOUND OF PACKING TAPE..............................215
HELLO. IT DOESN'T MATTER. 216

IX.
HOW THE BODY WORKS THE DARK

SUNLIGHT	221
MORE	222
SOON	224
OLD	225
MOP	226
SUNDAY	227
DAMN	228
CRUEL	229
MERCY	231
PALACE	232
I LOVE YOU	232
THE FIREPLACE	234

X.
LOVE ENDS IN A TANDEM KAYAK

END TIMES TIMELINE 239
A WETSUIT TOO TIGHT 241
QUIET AS A BURN PILE 243
ACCIDENTAL SUICIDE 246
HUNGER SLING 248
IN SWEATS, IN DEATH 250
CROOKED CONSTELLATIONS 252
MURDER OF THE MIDNIGHT JEWELER 255
WEIGHTED BLANKET 258
SMALL WINDOWS IN THE YOGA PANTS 259
BREEZE ADMISSION 261
THE FIRST KISS AS THE LAST KISS 263
PHLOX 264
I ALSO HATE SEEING A BABY IN A LEATHER MINI SKIRT .266
A MERCY MOST NATURAL 268
VISION BOARD 271
IT'S ALL COMEDY 273

ABOUT THE AUTHOR .... END

"One writes out of one thing only - one's own experience. Everything depends on how relentlessly one forces from this experience the last drop, sweet or bitter, it can possibly give. This is the only real concern of the artist, to recreate out of the disorder of life that order which is art."

-James Baldwin

GIVE UP THE SHIP SOMETIMES

NIGHT COLLAPSER

YOU AND ME AT PALACE LAKE

I want to dance poorly professionally,
feel my grief unwind
like a lie.

I want to see you laugh like a golden jackhammer,
feel you rattle my spine
into crumbs.

Do you think of me?
I keep thinking
of a little fish.

I don't want to die meaningless
flushed down
the slippery
 plumbing
of sadness.

I want to watch the sun
eat the lake with you,
feel the lake as one of us, fighting to remain endless.

I don't want to be another erasure,
a palace of violence, a trophy case
all fathers weep against.

The hungry grip of night is tightening
my scarf.
A lone tree on a hill catches too much lightning.

When I am a heft of alone,
alone feels like home.
Burn that home.

Lords of love,
strange design,
who dressed me up as an exit sign?

This lake realizes it is a dying lake, desperate
to maintain the last evaporating puddle, rain rewinding,
revealing the drying final floor of want,

and that fish, that one last fish
still swimming
in circles.

ODE TO THE PUBLIC PARK

The holy park by my Mom's house
holds all my firsts, tight as a nunchuk —
first bike ride, first fall, first bad kiss,
first taste of fearlessness. Torn porn, scabs and ramps.

The park taught me everything for teen excellence—
how to pop a wheelie like a drunk praise pastor,
how to ride my bike down the long tongue of the metal slide,
how to hold my tears while bleeding.

The tough kids gathered by the basketball court,
dressed like smoke, all pleather jackets and bad dreams,
while I practiced ollies until my shins bloomed
purple as summer plums, the crucial education of falling.

This was my first university:
I discovered the unknowable mathematics
of sneaky speed kissing on the creaking swings, *No one saw!*
All thin and nervous in the confused algebra of doomed-love.

Years later, when the world sits heavy,
a faded sailor anchor on my chest,
and every day burns me out like color evacuating a sunset,
I still come here.

Walk these worn paths quiet,
find the House Finch perched on the drinking fountain
unload my day upon her feathered shoulders—
she nods, knowing, flies away with all my gray luggage.

SHE COLLAPSED THE NIGHT

Can it all be as dumb as:
I saw you one day?
As simple as: I saw you one day?

I was a boring city, fading in my own gossip.
You were a marching band of bedazzled blue jeans.
You were a speaker blasting love back into science.
You were a fun pool. So many pools are shaped to remind us
only of the glory of the kidney, the comforting rectangle.
Why not give us a chaos grotto, a too-curvy slide,
a diving board that hurts children.
Something to do at a party. It's all we want.
You were a party with something to do
beyond wetting my throat and taunting the shrubs.

You were the pedal mashed to the floor, sticking.
You were the child allowed to stay up past bedtime
and mainline cake.
You were a funeral where everyone is forced to waltz alone.

How were you made?
Under a disco of starlight and rosemary brushfire?
Your eyes. Little flares. A gaze of rescue.

Your voice was the last and best chorus.
You were the place where terror came to lay down
and confess that it has been
a little spooky bitch.

Your kiss was fast medicine,
zipped into my gums.
Your skin is a museum of new snow.

Someday, you may walk without me
but you will never wander alone.
Hand to chest,
hold your breath,
there I am
at the bottom of the exhale.
You have come to soften the night.

Above a shivering world of
unaffordable studio apartments, future gloom and digital death,
I saw you one day-
humming some tiny frenzy,
something I longed to understand,
with the four remaining embers of desire.

I have let this heart work too long
for the party of muted safety.
I have let this heart sell all its favorite records
for cool, mumbling noise.

Even when I feel the nearness of that final inalterable lullaby,
when all sound begins to slip deeper underwater with age,
you are still my favorite song.

SUPERBLOOM

It is August and
the fires are ready
to fatten themselves again.

I miss living under clear skies on my boat,
safe and lonely swaying.
Little white birds
giving me morning.

I live under a god
who has thrown in the towel.

I want to leave the LA valleys of danger and feel a real
Portugal inside.
Portugal was the first place I felt like myself.
Like my voice sounded at ease, finally.
Portugal waits like a postcard of Portugal,
the one I keep writing
and tearing up
and writing again
because I like imagining a better future
without having to do the work
to go get it.

The distance between us grew
like a rumor
like a blooming tumor.

The photographs stopped coming.
The screens of us, black
as a confessional.

I come across as sudden weather
and I am exciting at first
but then it seems I have only come to fuck up your hair,
the annoyance of me trying to crack your little safe.

The problem is you see lovers like produce,
endless aisles of colorful possibility,
while I'm pretty sure everything's expired

and I want just the last piece
of good meat.

I hold the good memory inside:
You pale as wafers,
chuck wine drunk and laughing,
my mouth learning
the lost language
of your thin-ass collarbone,
your skin as warm as writer's block.

The only woman
in New Mexico not maimed
by a chainsaw.
You were too much teal.
Your lovely long arms, ristras from vigas.
Your lips all watermelon pink like the last
    sunset over the Sandias.

Oh man. Your hair. Dust devil mess, wild
tower, fresh skyline.

Life is a pause between lovers.

I just want to be 80/20,
80 percent good is good.

Why not just move away to Portugal and
fall in love with myself
or a soft idea in yoga pants
instead of buying an air purifier and
hunkering?
Why not find a place that doesn't
incinerate every year
instead of buying a better face mask?
Everyone is pretending the ash is snow and
all we really need are better skis.

I had a nightmare where I was dying with
a different voice. No one knew me
anymore.
I woke and didn't speak all day.

I roll down the car window
and release letters
to the California wind:
I just can't bring myself
to burn them.

Thin white useless birds that never learned to fly,
look like they're trying.

WATER THE POISON

When it's Tuesday
and the moon is as black and forgotten as   someone,
The Colossus Frequencies descend like French fog,
transmitting new fates to the newborns.

February boy
looks bloated on mystery hunger.
Let's spank his sloppy wet butt
and give this scrunched up milk junky some similes.
He will become his scovel-loving idol.
He will be a champagne flute full of poison.
Give him poetry for it will uncouple him
from his secrets
soon enough.

Have you accepted the fate assigned by the Colossus?

I am nearing that age when my father found madness.
Blessed be the Colossus and this holy inheritance:
The hot peppers of Papa, rising through my throat
like a buried transmitter finally receiving my future gospel.

Mama's full wardrobe of surrender flags,
bleached and written into my nervous system
like commandments in bone.

Thou shalt often say, God said it, I believe it and that settles it.
Thou shalt not daydream thyself into misery.
Thou shalt not research the fear rooted in a garage filled with bottled
    water.
Thou shalt water down the wine with ice.
Thou shalt worry about drowning all the time.
Thou shalt love your boy
and wonder when he will grow out of his mistrust and doubt of the
    Colossus.

I have been ordained to
permanent member of the Royal Order
of Party Corner Surveillance.
When I blaspheme that the chemtrails over Texas

are the Colossus's skidmarks
the divine voice reminds me I am not a jester,
I am an instrument of prophecy and smash.

The Colossus taught me humidity control,
to pull weather
from the audience's eyes but did not teach me
how to be likable.
Ten writers read their work out loud in one night.
Someone learns that all writing is a collection of small panics
The top-selling book is based on whoever the audience wishes they were.

I am to be seen as a suffering thing
that sells pieces of the suffering thing like a Costco sample.

When T-Mobile asks me about my day
I go into great detail:
my Father is dying, my stepfather is dying, my friends are dying, rent
    went up
and now they want me to pay with my soul and won't allow me to do a
    fiddle playing challenge instead…
and when they tell me to pray about it
Hold please… and punch the couch twenty times,
fuck fuck fuck…
"Mr. Brown?"
Sorry. I thought I hung up.
"You didn't. Have you eaten today? Praise Colossus."
I have not eaten. Praise Colossus.

I become what I swore I would water down.

I ask everyone at the party what they're drinking
and if they believe in the Colossus of THE COLLOSUS
or if its just a conspiracy? What if the thing above is very small?
When a woman who smells, 'delivery food good,' tries to show me
    warmth…

it's magic time-
I disappear into my phone.

I am lactose and all horned up
and eat 3 slices of pizza at the party so I can get sick
and leave early.
I tell the host "I gotta go cause I'm tired inside my mouth."
I got weird like my Pops used to get weird at parties.
I shoulda started a conversation instead of posing
on the lawn like a yawn.

I want to be a new thing.
I want to feel my body tingle as it erases itself from yearbooks and
reunion photos. I fight the Colossus until it is undone.

Tomorrow
I want to fight and at least get one win.
When I fight and win,
I speak to the waiter like a friend and make eye contact when they arrive.
I ask someone curt, what they meant instead of volcanoing all my
      peppers.
I show up on time and widen my business handshake arm into something
      more
comprehensively two-armed and embarrassingly friendly.
I invite you for dinner and when you flake
I eat your portion and lay fat and tell you its cool.
I answer truthfully when you ask about my day —
instead of doing the writer thing, I fight to look outward,
knowing you had weather too,
you got some Colossus raining down
you got a bad haircut and cried
you're hurting
you got pals dying too
you got me realizing I don't need to fill
every silence with my impression of a knobless stereo.

I am choosing to be powerfully softer now,
the watered-down blood is trying.
I'm trying.
I keep the hose in the bowl,
keep adding fresh water to the poison
until everyone can drink.

YOU CAN SUE THE HORIZON

I can't cry at movies anymore cause the HD
left me no room to wonder.
I don't want my life to be a great trailer but a bad film.
I don't want to be subtitled on the cheap
cause no one understands the language of my hunger.
In all this not-wanting
lives a wanting so fizzy it scares me to open —

Can I live a life of tiny retaliations?

May I rip a fart into every landlord's envelope,
mail back eviction notices full of loose glitter? Grazie.
You drive a cop car into my neighborhood,
you're getting googly eyes on it. Right in the O!
Death has been texting me 5 times a day. Get over us.
It's time to reserve my tombstone that says, "living my best life."

Go ahead, get in the elevator,
I'm not turning around to face the same way as everyone.
Look at me. Look at the new me. Don't you dare mention the weather.
No more talking about the weather,
when the weather should be talking about me.
No more people telling Derrick to sign a receipt to make it legal.
I am only signing my name as a cloud.
Come and sue the horizon! You will lose.

This is the year I force everyone to finally circle back to me
after they said,
"Let's circle back on that."

Allow me to write confusing Yelp reviews to all my heartbreakers:
"Nice lighting. Clean dining area. Can't French right.
No manager here. I saw bugs. Two stars."

From this day forth, you're not a little shit wizard anymore, Derrick.
You're a wizard-wizard. A MAGICAL THING.
So why can't you remember to cast at least one useful spell?
Why have you been the king of dumb spells?
Why is it always, abracadabra, make this menu shorter?
Abracadabra, make this person stop telling me about their dream.

Abracadabra, make this loneliness more lesson
and less long WiFi password paranoia.

How many more days will you waste your power?

Derrick! Why can't you play guitar sad enough to earn a house?
Why won't you learn to find the smell of jasmine
when you are insecure? Why are you insecure? You're hot.
No one makes a credit card feel more used up than you,
you little gutterslut.

Why won't you cast the spell that makes you stop needing everyone
to think you're funny
before they're allowed to think you're infinitely human?

How about you stop organizing your books by color
like some Magnolia Farms fanboy,
stop arranging salvation by shade.
Why won't you finally get off your ass and organize your books by
    subject?
The whole organizing your books by color thing
makes it look like you never run to your bookshelf
like it's a medicine cabinet, an ammunition depot,
panting in cold sweat and loss,
urgently needing some good words downrange to stay in the fight.
Marie Howe next to Self defense?
End of times Survival manuals next to Terrance Hayes? yep.
You got too many books you never let inside

You don't have much time!
The era for caution and tenderness is over.
No more pretending you don't need help.
No more tiptoes and digital handshakes,
no more trusting anyone on Instagram who takes pretty food pictures
without telling me where to get it.
No more nodding along when people say, "Everything happens for a
    reason."
Eat shit and choke on a vision board you ethereal fuck.
I'm loving my beautifully painful, random life.

I'm tired of being a good little wizard for the machine,
All this American billionaire boot stomp and performed gratitude for
　　scraps
and there's still nowhere to piss,
nowhere to sleep without selling your blood,
nowhere that doesn't demand you shut your mouth
so you can keep your job and die scared.
I have stored too many small miracles
in a colander.

No more.
I'm saying… small magic ain't enough now to make it to next year.
We gotta go big now.
You are going to have to sacrifice something you love,
to keep this freedom you love.

If we make it to next year,
let's stop casting spells for the masters,
start conjuring revolutions in the backrooms.

Turn our creativity and magic toward the throat of the gimmes.
It's time to go big. Time for insane spells.
What's insane? Admit we need each other to make it through.

　　　Help.　　Learn　　to　　say　　Help.

I'm asking you to do something insane,
if you see me,
if we make it to next year,
do something totally insane,
hold me tight.

WEDDING POEM 15
for Dylan and Kristen

I have been to 14 weddings
that tried to tell me love was patient,
love was kind,
and those people are idiots.

I think I finally got a pin on what love may be.
It is dressing up real nice and going nowhere.
It is a lazy tornado of comforters and staying in for the night.
Love is two people's laundry mixing together and no one is pissed.
Love is desperate to get me to put on roller skates after two beers.

Love isn't a home. It's the hammer that builds the home.

When love holds fast, your wedding doesn't have to be the same:
Some parent mad that someone like me is the officiant
and demanding I include at least one bible verse
and I always choose the fun one.

Deuteronomy 23:1, "No one whose testicles are crushed
or whose male organ is cut off shall enter the assembly of the Lord
because these are new carpets."

Your wedding doesn't have to always be dry chicken
and people begging the DJ to play dumb shit
 and toasts where Uncle Gene made it about Vietnam again.
Can we applaud the flower girl meltdown?
Can you blow a smoke circle when the priest asks for the ring?
Love ain't a perfect day captured in a carousel of good light,
love is getting sick and not being scared,
it is soup when I need some god damned soup.

It ain't gotta be all spanx and shoes that hurt to mambo #5 in.
Some cheddar faced photographer
hollering at grandma to "forget every challenge you've witnessed"
and smile big!

They tried to tell me love was finding your other half,
your soulmate, your completion guide,
but love is an oh no what the fuck is happening, I give up.
Love is the sound waves of the ballad bouncing off my metal fillings.
Love is permanent mercy in a world that rations kindness.
Love is a swim partner through a universe
of lonely phantoms and soft madness.
Love is 2 AM al pastor tacos,
a hand hold when I am as lonely as the west,
spontaneous cocktails that taste like LA air,
the hours when I forget the world exists beyond your collarbone.

Love is the last slice of pizza neither of us wants to take.
Love is the one you call as the world ends.
Love is a funeral where everyone tells the truth.
Love is your hands knowing exactly where I hid my fractures.
Love is us fucking like it could close down a religion.
Love is us saying each other's names
like they're the only words left.

I DON'T KNOW HOW TO SAY MY INSIDES
for Alex and Hannah and their little battalion

Alex tells his daughters
he has only 40 summers left, max.
In those glee-gloss beach naps and afternoons
of chucking balls to dogs,
maybe 14 unforgettable days.

I have six great days left to live.
So I will give away the three wishes I won in a foxhole miracle.
I will spend all six days as a pastor in a pub, awarding the deserved.

It's a bar full of accidental fathers.

I ask for a show of hands for who fucked up.
The tall ones catch their arms in the ceiling fans.

Tell me.

The short guy says, "Most of the men I have been are fictional."
Bahama shirt says, "I never thanked any of the fish I killed and ate."
Sportsman says, "I have never finished a sad book."
Long shorts says, "I give my daughters sugar
before dropping them off at their mothers."
Then, the broest of bros says,
"I don't know... how to say my insides."

I feel for the guy. I give him my best wish and he shakes violently upon
    chugging it, then says,

"I can see. I swear I once felt something powerful inside
and I killed it when I turned 13.
There are wants now, that power, coming down the wire."

I motion for him to continue, "Tell us them wants, buddy."

"I think I want… to know the places alive beyond the places I know.
The heaving Malabar Coast.
The hum of Sri Lanka.

Cinnamon trees,
how their powders calm my blood.
I don't know what I am supposed to look like, but it isn't this.
I don't want to see my body as a grief machine.
I want to be kind as candelight.
Fucking didn't earn me much but temporary scary scary.
And fixing up my car took so much of my life. I want that time back.
I drink so much to drown the noise of all my promise.
I want to follow little dangers back to their apartments
and travel in a long pressure of madness.
I can tell I'd like a very filthy love
and to someday live where I wear out all the things I have
before replacing them.
Why are you weeping, Derrick?"

"Oh no," I say, "I'm so sorry. I think I just ruined your life.
I think you're a Goddamned writer."

FULL METAL NECKLACES 2
for Andrea Gibson

You are laughing up moths,
bleeding in your boy pants,
breathing your poems out
like burning garlands.

Soon,
a woman from the audience,
full of woe and strange posture,
is crying on you.

I watch your hands sheath themselves
into your safe back pockets.
You're not sure what to say
or how to hold all of this woman.

I don't know what kind of advice
can make the anchors
in your fan's neck
go away.

Closer. The woman is a girl.
When her crying slows,
your arms wrap around Girl
as if someone is going to steal her skin.

You hang there
like a constellation settling into its own wide black.
Looks like she is holding you up.
She is. You're so skinny.

A young girl slung around your neck,
snot and tears
staining your boring sweatshirt.
So many more to embrace. So many more sweatshirts to ruin.

We are necklaces,
dipped in your voice-box,
shining metal struggle,
crazed and heavy around you.

Your gay sweatshirt,
a traveling canvas,
painted in the unfurling mess
of us.

Your poems growl for the living
because you hear the dying gray ones,
hear them so clearly,
unsure of how to whisper out the medicine, so you roar in color.

I used to tell people poetry is hidden
in everything.
You showed us that it isn't hiding.
It is waiting.

Just waiting for someone to call it on a Thursday night
or ask it over for chili
or hold it tightly until it can wipe its nose
and catch its breath.

SLOW THE BURN
for Melanie

At the Roger Room on La Cienega,
the bourbon clocks in and does its job.
A small pour, dum-dum time machine,
summoning fire to the voice box.
We tweak each other's work. She's a good Texan.

I turn the amber in my glass, ice ticking like a metronome.
Memory, scram.

"What do you wish you wrote about more?"

That I am grateful when I survive sleep.
Grateful for cold movie theaters on tour days off
and jackets I forgot that I hid in the car.
Glad for all the basement reading sweat fests
where I witnessed authors transform into surgeons of air.

Glad I made it out of the paratrooper job alive.
All those airplanes I stepped from, smooth tubes of war,
a world spread below like sheets of hammered emerald,
the vastness of sky consuming me with a blue mouth.
Grateful that the death horse I saw coming for me sprained its ankle.

Grateful for the countless times I said yes
to the meandering scenes of love's confusion,
each moment of tour sex; a private surrender,
a chance to take their secrets with me outta town.

One night, my pal wanted our motel room
for him and his date
and I roamed Myrtle Beach
and someone left a sun-bleached beach chair and Mexican blanket
and I was so glad, me and the chair hauled in the dawn, staring
like an almost widow, waiting for my husband's ship.

"How about you?"

"Less about men. Ya'all are so terrible."

"Do you still have a boyfriend?"

"Of course. Know your enemy."

"Preach", I said.

"Why do we do this, Derrick?
Drain ourselves empty for a little release of the weight?"
Why document what will soon be forgotten? Who asked for this?
Who needs another rain story in a drowning world?
Why prove we existed by writing? What do we win from the odd pull of sharing? What does this proof of life get us?

"I dunno," I say.

Melanie says. "Can we talk about the previous stanza?
I am not sure I ever said those things.
But I could see you having me say those things to serve your poem.
Keep critiquing my piece, and don't be precious.
Poems don't have always to be fantastical. Just say the thing."

Then, I swear, I see the fireplace reach towards the whiskey and ask, "Can you put me out?"
And the thing in the glass that can burn, that can satisfy or kill, answers:

In a way.

READ THIS TO THE OLD MAN
for Russ Tamblyn

It shouldn't scare me to say I love you, Old Man,
but the words stick like apple labels.
Hearing it back, that's some knife.
I've been dodging those words since I learned
to make myself small.

I thought Old Man love tells you to zip it,
a love that never mentions itself,
an uh-oh rising in my throat.
Old Man love is supposed to sprawl out on the couch and ignore you,
a love that knows when to shut up.
Why do you have to make me hear you say it? Sincere, clear and easy.

I used to believe God wore my father's dissapointed face,
kept a ledger
of bad grades
and the blood
I couldn't scrub
from under my fingernails.

Strange how looking backward makes it so hard to run.

I hope good memories come gentle and warm you into sleep,
through mountain smoke and crisp palm trees,
through California's blue-dream hours.

Your stories unspool like film reels, Russ,
all those faces signing their names in the mind:
the dead, the disappeared, the loved ones
who burned too bright to stick around.

Sometimes I watch you—
imagine your heart as an overstuffed suitcase,
soaked in whiskey and celluloid light,
bursting at the latches.

Full as a loaded paintbrush hovering
over white canvas, trembling
with all that color it hasn't spilled yet.

I see you: tarantula tamer, horror strainer,
the gymnast who somersaulted through the nightmare
and stuck the landing on both feet, grinning.

You are not just a snapping Jet,
not just the kid who could pull a full-nelson on gravity.

Not just a wild doctor, not just a Dracula killer,
not a sea Captain clutching his whiskey cup like a compass,
not a priest tallying sins in the confessional dark,
not an old God sharpening knives for the lamb,
not the love interest, not the drug, not the man-shark baring his teets,
not the minute hand's small surrender.

You are dust and spit and miracle to me,
present tense, walking around in leather sandals and black socks, a middle finger to fashion,
a mouth that pours love out like an ointment.

When I look at you, I'm trying to memorize
a little beautiful boring thing:
your face before the story starts. Mid air.
I see, in your eyes, you have lived your ass off. Your mistakes
took their shots but couldn't drop you.

Didn't you love until your clothes
split into rags of surrender?
Yelled until your tongue went all droopy,
rolled and danced until sweat turned to gold,
loved so hard, we reach our hands toward the slow fire of you?
This is one way to get through.

Old Man, we're down to our last few songs.
The band's packing their horns.
Soon the house lights, brutal and fluorescent,
will warm on down.

Press your ear to this page, old man.
Down here in the small print...
I love you, friend. I love your love
and its uncomplicated machinery:
a handshake that means it,
a door held open in the rain.

MY JOB IS MAKING SENSE

My chest tightens like a childhood pageant sash when I think of squeezing the grand prize out of you, your puffed rice kiss, oh-to-be-body-checked playing tonsil hockey. Come to me now. Hair is the hourglass of love. I don't have much time. How is this country still so dumb, even though everyone bought a smart bed? I wish we made sense for a living. I wish this world made more sense. I wish there were more brown toilets, toilet seat holes weren't for giants, blood-colored scrubs only for nurses, and no one is allowed to wear white shoes anymore, so I don't have to see how proud they are of how busy they've been. You make this world make ten percent more sense. The wind hushes across the ocean of moons and the seas are calm again. I can do nothing with you and feel like everything is happening. Let's be as stupid as these times. Let's learn the courage found in a pun. And why are so many in this word afraid of the big bad pun. And how am I not a doctor? Cause I've been surgeon for you all my life.

TWEEN SPIRIT

"Is this Mr. Brown?"
"This is he."
"You weren't seen in school today."
"I was there."
"Not saying you weren't there. But you weren't seen."

A GLASS PAGEANT

Afternoon unfolds its gray wool over the lake
as I row the boat deeper into its center.

The daffodil wind swoops.
My arm hairs stiffen in the chill like little skinny possums.

Rich Hippies wave from their decks,
prog-rock humming through their bones.
Do you like these jams? I am curious these days. But only so much.
No thanks! I only understand songs that have a foundational ache!

Their free-spirited smiles unroll like white-bleached beach blankets.
One haunts the jank of guitar strings, another sings of his favorite smell,
and they call me to row over. Drum circle free love.
They all pause to honor the death of a shooting star.
I am hesitant to engage.
I am hesitant to bring my little machine around them.

This machine in my pocket is warming.
I want to tell them what this little machine does to people.

When the talk grows quiet, I press the button.
Our skins slip away like silk gowns, hushing the floor.
We peel like orange rinds.
We are horrified and then laugh, wet and red-dripping underflesh.
Veins braided, countdown timers glowing on our hearts,
little time bombs.

Shame and mistake badges, plucked from our sinew like burrs.

We climb back into our skins, divers into strange wetsuits.
Some faces are set wrong: eyes too low,
smiles crooked as broken plates glued lazily.

The moon yawns open its sharp jaw.

Why did you do that to us, Derrick?
Someone reaches for the guitar but the fingers won't remember.

The hippie jams won't arrive from their throats, thought they try.
Now they only know a new posession,
minor chords, songs that bend and break,
ballads of molasses and loss—each note a small funeral,
each lyric an apology and a begging for mercy.
Their countdown timers tick in rhythm.
The sorrowful metronome. They play until dawn,
and I row home through their keening,
oars cracking the water like fresh peanut brittle,
the machine cooling like a spent shell in my pocket.

COLOSSUS OF NEVER

The mobile home is being shredded
by the 20th tropical depression this year
and there wasn't enough money for a basement
and they should have scrubbed the tub that they hunkered and prayed in.

The storm takes no requests.

They all die.

When the high tides of blood and suffering come like a leather cloak,
a screech on repeat,
one person always finds my ear and tells me,
"We will never know God's plan—
but he knows what is best and
sometimes offers us trials that we will suffer through to test our faith."

No. Not like this.

We don't suffer because we stray. We suffer when we refuse truth.
He may help. He may choose not to. We don't get to know.
But it doesn't hurt to ask for help.

Yes it does.

I once saw my father try to earthquake the demons and teeth out of my
    mother.
I low crawled and stole the checkbook when we left.
He came to the door and saw us as we put the car in neutral
to roll out of the driveway quietly.

*I don't know why God is letting this happen
but I trust he has a plan.*

Us as children staring, hours later,
"When is Daddy coming to meet us?"

Little kids.
Little kids worshipping the dark colossus of never.

BOMB THREAT CHECKLIST 2
provided by Corporate Security

STEP 1: QUESTIONS TO ASK:

1. When is the bomb going to explode?
2. Where is the bomb right now? Riddles stress me out.
3. What does it look like? Is it pretty?
4. What kind of bomb is it? Is there a brand name on the bomb?
5. What will cause the bomb to explode? Is there something explosive in the bomb?
6. Did you place the bomb? Did anyone you love place the bomb?
7. Why? (If suspect responds with 'why not', give suspect 10 reasons why you enjoy life. (Edit down to 3 reasons if he sounds serious. It will be a He.)
8. What is your address? How does it feel to recall your first phone number?
9. What is your name? Can I call you, Bud?
10. What does your name mean?
11. How does fire make you feel?

STEP 2: LISTEN FOR CALLER'S VOICE. IS IT:

Calm angry excited slow loud Motherly
stutter familiar stutter recognized?

(If caller sighs, mark "tired." If caller hums, mark "suspiciously melodic." If caller chokes, mark "possibly too many necklaces for my taste.")

STEP 3: LISTEN FOR THREAT LANGUAGE. IS IT:

Well spoken foul irrational taped
before a live studio audience rock steady—
Is he asking you to the prom or to the bomb? Q-tips!

Ask him to enunciate, and when he asks you
to spell it, spell it ANNUNCIATE and he will say
that means to announce like an angel blowing horns,
saying the end times are near and that's when you
mark your sheet, "hallelujah."

STEP 4: LISTEN FOR BACKGROUND SOUNDS.
ARE THERE:

Street noises voices animal noises factory machinery
the sound of heat voices embers motors static voices?

Do you hear an office paper shredder,
sobbing at all the ideas dying?

Do you hear the dull hum of someone attaching
themselves to their saddest moment?

Do you hear a minutehand counting down
to Stop-pretending-o-clock?

Do you hear a dog sniffing that refuses
to belong to anyone?

Do you hear the clack of heels that are actually panic
in sensible shoes?

Then mark the sheet: POSSIBLE: factory / backyard /
furnace / someone's last good joke writing spot /
ritualized despair.

Circle "unknown," if comfortable with that word.

STEP 5: LISTEN FOR THE EXACT WORDING
OF THE THREAT

Does he speak like someone who has learned
to love his cracked phone screen for what it has been through
and still working?

Does he sound on the verge of yelling:
"mama say, mama saw mamakoosaw"—?
Does it sound like an 'end of my rope' incantation
you would use to mend a dress
or call a dog who refuses to be named?

Does he sound like he knows how far a person
can be pushed before the seam rips?

Does he know the exact timeline it took for him
to touch the wall of madness?

Do what you are trained to do:
be efficient, be professional, be polite,
don't think, follow the rules—
trust the paperwork.

If there is an explosion,
raise a glass as the fires of love sing down.
Red wine of course.
Goes good with meat.

HOUSE OF NEW LANGUAGE
for Jennifer

It's at jellyfish speed,
it's a sand shark tail whip when you kiss me.

I bend before you like grass stomped by the search party.
It hits first like cooling booze, sunlight trapped in a swimming pool.

You are an education in desire.
The way you push me up against the fridge, the poor food.

I love my tongue sorting the quality Canadian healthcare in your teeth.
I love being
velveted in your lips.
Your breasts pull me into the little kickdrum below. You beat different.
You make this world feel less lonely.
I am in love with your dance in big socks. My baby snakes. My
international super baby.
 I love how alone you love the morning.

I love watching you love your morning.
I love all the former smoke in your laugh.
You are the girl on the stool in the bar next to me, mangling me up.
You are not right.
Goddamned beautiful beyond what is supposed to be.

Hotel inside a fortress,
you are a second summer right after the first.
My nakedness spills into yours.
I wish you were a backpack.

I know your loneliness now and I'm not afraid.
We kiss and say, "It's good to meet you, is someone sitting here?"

A cinema of night falls and we tangle fingers,
your body becomes a found story.

How do I become your sweat?
Your blonde everything.

Love's merciful lightning is killing everything outside.
You are why I want and why I want to come home.

BORN IN THE YEAR
OF THE BUTTERFLY KNIFE

THE KUROSAWA CHAMPAGNE

Tonight
your body shook,
hurling your nightmares
back to Cambodia.

Your nightgown wisped off
into Ursa Minor.

I was left here on earth feeling alone,
paranoid about the Rapture.

Tonight,
I think it is safe to say we drank too much.
Must I apologize for the volume in my slobber?
Must I apologize for the best dance moves ever?
No.
Booze is my tuition to clown college.
I swung at your purse.
It was staring at me.

We swerved home on black laughter,
bleeding from forgettable boxing.

I asked you to sleep in the shape of a trench
so that I might know shelter.

I drew the word surrender in the mist of your breath,
waving a white sheet around your body.
'Dear, in the morning let me put on your make-up for you.
I'll be loading your gems with mascara
then I'll tell you the truth…'
I watched black ropes and tears ramble down your face.
Lady war paint.
A squad of tiny men rappels down those snaking lines
and you say;
"Thank you for releasing all those fuckers from my life."

You have a daily pill case.
There are no pills inside.
It holds the ashes of people who died

…the moment they saw you.

The cinema we built was to play the greats,
but we could never afford the power
so in the dark cinema
you painted pictures of Kurosawa.
I just stared at you like Orson Welles,
getting fat off your style.

You are a movie that keeps exploding.
You are Dante's fireplace.

We were so broke,
I'd pour tap water into your mouth,
burp against your lips
so you could have champagne.
You love champagne.

Sparring in the candlelight.
Listen—
the mathematical equivalent of a woman's beauty like yours
is directly relational
to the amount or degree
other women hate her.
You, dear, are hated.

Your boots are a soundtrack to adultery.
Thank God your feet fall in the rhythms of loyalty.

If this feeling kills me,
slice me open, julienne,
uncurl my veins
and fashion yourself a noose
so I can hold you
once more.

HOT FOR SORROW

When the police helicopters showed up,
I grabbed onto the skid
and they flew me cross town
to your house.
I watched you through the glass as you slept
like jewelry in a coffin.

I screamed out,
"Hey!
I don't want to be the best lover you've ever had,
I just want to be your favorite."
There's a difference.

File me under hot for sorrow.

When I couldn't find your picture,
I ate unwanted videotapes and dreamt.
When you appeared, soft-focused,
outlined in lasers,
embarrassed of your little T-Rex arms and seaweed hair,
we danced on the ceiling like Lionel Richie
until it was time to walk you home
from naked class. A+.

This cross-eyed sniper
misses you so much.

The heavy solo night music
tells me what powers our city:

Ambulances hooked on one ballad–
A sky turning red over its opponents.
Night melodies of helicopter switchblades
slice through this city.
The noise tells me there is still crime down there.
5000 air machines cannot stop crime.
5000 searchlights cannot stop crime.

5000 police fully mustached,
and our names on every baton
cannot stop crime.

I now know that what I feel for you is crime.

This is why I like the sound of police choppers:
not because it makes me feel safe and watched over
but rather because the sound is the music of war,
and tonight
they were playing our war.

AQUANAUT

Downtown Long Beach is a woman
packed with heavy ghosts
in heavy coats
who aches when the gulls pass through her.

She is woman, surrounding us in night fog,
loosening our tourniquets with sultry mist,
healing wounds by directing embraces to the gasses of starlight.

Tonight, a telescope points toward her high-rise fingers,
spying the open windows for the last place God hid my ignition,
for the last place I tangled the sex in your shadow.

Tonight, there are no knives.
No reason to pull the razorblade
out from behind the library card in your wallet.

No reason to soar from the green spine
of the Vincent Thomas bridge.

No reason to collapse
in the rusted regret dumpster
behind the Reno Room on Broadway.

Orion awaits over Avalon.

Remember how we wanted to water ski there,
all the way to the island
on the backs of the aquarium bat-rays?

And remember how I haggled the rays into it
by giving them back their stingers?
And remember how hard you kissed me
as we mounted onto their slime and leather wings?
And remember how the rays swerved us recklessly
through the Pacific oil rig pylons?

And remember how the sensation made you feel so close to death
which made us feel more alive?

We raced under wide Catalina stars
until the lights over Pine Street called us home
to a tired sailboat harbor
where masts creak and sway like a brigade of crosses
marching nowhere.

You said, Let's steal the Queen Mary!
We'll watch her sweep through the August glow of red tides
Drinking in the tiny green fireflies of the sea.

I told you your kiss made me feel like Winston Churchill
and you said- powerful?
and I said- drunk.

Today the Queen is at rest-still unmoved,
rusted, boilers removed, gutted and ready to live.

I spend my days looking for anchors,
plotting courses to deserted ports,
attaching more telescopes to my sailboat
in hopes that I will catch that siren
combing her fingers through the shocks of hair
that falls from her head like thousands of wet rosaries.

Slow halo-generator woman of Long Beach—
I will watch and wait for the look to return to your face—
The look you used to give as an Aquanaut close to death
Head rocked back
Eyes pinched full of twilight and drunk fantasy.

When the morning laughs out loud with big teeth,
When the asphalt smells like a melting Buddhist,

the devotion-the prayer-the heat-all you.
I know that the city holds you as one of its lost.
Lost for now—
never forever.

WHY AMELIA EARHART WANTED TO VANISH

Amelia asks for forgiveness,
looks down at the table like we are playing chess.
The larger pout of her bottom lip is imported from
Uruguay: Ooo—doo—guy.

Her R's and the A's become dizzy ghosts when she says it.
Distance.
The bottom lip
simple as a sentence.
But the upper lip,
a complex creature.

Amelia's youth-suitcased in the upper lip-ready for wrinkles.
Lipstuck lipstick lipstock residue in flushed hue
like she'd been kissing madly,
like she walked off the set of an MGM ending
cast to kiss sailors ready to die.

Some are ready to die.
Her hair looks as if she'd been running with a man in black and white
through the sets of dangerous cities.
Her few hard lines are just symptoms of sleeping on her face,
Amelia ruins pillowcases with her lipstick.

Zip focus into the darkness where her lips should meet.
God, Those corners.
The black pockets-empty and full
like poverty.

These are not simple.
Endless. Hungry. Surrounded.
Dragging air like jets of the atmosphere.
Drawing it in
in slow motion,
drawing it in freehand
into those corner lip pockets.
The separations open and close,
move elastic in melody with her chest.
1,2,3,4, 1,2,3,4 1…
Air marches in

and then nothing more marches out.

I could low-crawl inside those corner pockets,
grab her gums
see if they're bleeding,
to see if she wondered if she said the right thing,
to see if there was some sign of wonder or weakness or nervous,
the way dogs watch everyone nervously after they've been hit by cars.

A sign that speaks of all normal persons having fear,
a bite in the cheek-a grind in the crowns
something that will give her away…
"C'mon Amelia. Come on. This is not chess, Amelia."
She says, "Shh. Save your yelling for sex and riots."

Peeking at the daylight from the corners of her mouth.
The dryness chaps.
I look for bats
or sailors' initials
but nothing.
For now it is dead in here.
The fifth of July.
January second,
December twenty sixth, etc.

I wait under the quilt of her tongue.
Unthawed.
Searching for blood.
Carving letters on her canines.
"Amelia. If you leave, don't you ever come back."
Alone in the cockpit, her propellers began to spin.

12:55

You never thought a human hand could look like this.
Desert cracks.
Folds brought together by age.
Your fingertips slide across this fortune teller's nightmare.

You notice the bruised knuckles from the years he drove his fists into the walls
looking for answers.
The hands of a captain who lost the entire sea.

Now the smell enters you:
The air conditioning ducts pumping medicine,
The people of white aprons, their shoulders raised from the cold
and the motionless silver goodnight machines.
The cold, the white aprons, the blood and tools,
reminders of science class and butcher shops.

It hits you that this building,
this room
was someone's last
toilet handle,
last pillow,
their last press on the power button
of a faded black remote control.

You feel sorry for the nurse that lost the draw and had to make the call;
"You must come now. The doctor says 1-2 days tops."
You lean down.
His eyes haunt and float between two worlds.
He is your father,

and you can't stop seeing him carrying you on his back
through the blink of youth.
"I'd take ya for a piggyback ride kiddo…but I think it would kill me."
You laugh. He coughs. You wait.
His eyebrows lift.
They are your eyebrows.
Head tilts to see your face,
"Ya know, if there's one thing I wish I would've done in my life,
I wish I would've spent more time at the office, for you."

"Really, Dad?"
"Of course not, you moron. Don't be so moronic…
Drink your coffee son. Don't waste it."
"You got me, Pop."
"Well, it's about time."

The clock hands at 12:55 A.M. look like they're surrendering,
and you think to yourself—
'This is bad coffee. My God, probably the worst.
How can they give him this shit?
Don't they know who he is?'

You drink it cause you get to drink together,
and you hold his hand
wondering if anyone would notice
if you took him from this place
on your back.

JOIN THE AIRBORNE

I asked my Drill Sergeant why our foxholes needed to be so deep.

"When an enemy grenade lands in the foxhole
that you dug six feet deep, the shrapnel will not destroy
any other men or equipment. When the enemy sends a
ball of fire through your fat head,
we don't have to worry about burying your
sorry ass cause you've already done the work for us."

Sounds good.

A Drill Sergeant used to tell me when he would be absent
so the squad leaders
could beat up the 'ate up' privates.
We beat up a guy who wet his bed before
inspection. His name was Middleton, I think. I'm so sorry. I was glass.

All men on our side of the base.
Going for weeks without even seeing a real woman
makes you want to kill even more.

I remember when a new paratrooper caught wind
into the training tower. His chute
collapsed and he straddled the metal.
Eighty feet up, he wept in pain and we
joked to the fire department, "save his balls"
cause there was nothing else we could do.

During basic training, a friend from L.A. in my unit
tried to kill himself by
trimming his dog tags and jamming them into a light socket.
I forget his name.
Maybe Stone.

At every base is a main flagpole with a ball on top called a truk.
It contains
A razorblade, a bullet and matches.
It is for the commander of the base, if over-
run, to climb to the top, cut up the flag, burn it and blow his brains out.
The 82nd has a marquee near Bastogne street.

It has a number on it.
If we could make it 82 days without a training accident
we could have a day off.
We hadn't had a day off in 10 years.

Because of the large increase in suicides near Christmas time
for members of the 82nd,
the base hired a NY choreographer to do a musical
based on making
soldiers feel good about being alive.
I was in it. We sang Memory from Cats
and We Got a Lot of Livin' To Do from some play.
It was ridiculous. It was one
more thing we did for show.
Soldier Safety Show. So much doesn't make sense.

Walking through airports in beret, jump boots and secrets,
I have never felt so proud.

TOMB

love is the only war worth dying for.

A FINGER, TWO DOTS, THEN ME

Lying together in the park on Seventh,
our backs smoosh grass and I say
I will love you till I become a child again,
when feeding me and bathing me
is no longer romantic,
but rather necessary.

I will love you till there is no till.
Till I die.

And when that electroencephalogram shuts down, baby,
that's when the real lovin' kicks in.

Forgive me for sounding selfish,
but I won't be able to wait under the earth for you
(albeit a romantic thought for groundhogs,
gophers and the gooey worms).

I will not be able to wait for you…
but I will meet up with you
and here's where you will find me:
get a pen—

Hold your finger up
(two fingers if your hands are frail by now)
and count two stars directly to the left
of the North American moon.
You will find me there.
You will find me darting behind amazing quasars,
Behind flirtatious winks
of bright and blasting boom stars!
Sometimes charging so far into space
the darkness goes
blue.

I will be there chasing sound waves
riding them like two-dollar pony ride horses
that have finally broken free and wild.
I will be facing backwards, lying sideways,
no hands, sidesaddle, sometimes standing,

sometimes screaming zip zang zowie!
My God, it's good to be back in space...Where is everybody?

You will recognize my voice.
You will see the flash of a fire trail
burning off the back of me
burning like a gasoline comet kerosene sapphire.
This is my voice.
Don't look for my body or a ghost.
I'll resemble more a pilot light than a man now.

I'm sure some will see
this cobalt star white light from earth
and cast me a wish like a wonder bomb.
And I'll think "Hmmph. People still do that. Good."
I'm sure I'll take the light wonder bombs
to the point in the universe
where sound does end.
The back porch of God's summer home.
It's so quiet, you float.
It feels the way cotton candy tastes.

I say to him...why do I call you God?
He says, 'Because Grand Poobah sounds ridiculous.'
I knew you had a sense of humor. I've been to Phoenix.

I ask him, 'Lord, so many poets have tried to nail it-
Ginsberg, Corso, and missed.
What is holy? What is actually holy?'
At that moment,
the planets begin to spin and awaken
and large movie screens appear on Mars, Saturn and Venus,
each bearing images I have witnessed
and over each and every clip flashes the word
holy.

armadillos—holy
magic tricks—holy
cows' tongues—holy
snowballs upside the head—holy
clumsy first kisses—holy
sneaking into the movies—holy

your mother teaching you to slow dance
the fear returning
the fear overcome—holy
eating top ramen on upside-down frisbees
cause it was either buy plates or more beer—holy
beach cruiser nights—holy
the $5.00 you made in Vegas
and the $450.00 you lost—holy
the last time you were nervous holding hands—holy
feeling God at a pool hall but not church—holy
sleeping during your uncle's memorized dinner prayer—holy
losing your watch in the waves and all that signifies—holy
the day you got to really speak to your father cause the television broke—
    holy
the day your grandmother told you something meaningful
cause she was dying—holy
the medicine
the hope
the blood
the fear
the trust
the crush
the work
the loss
the love
the test
the birth
the end
the finale
the design
in the stars
is the same
in our hearts
the design
in the stars
is the same
in our hearts
in the rebuilt machinery of our hearts

So love, you should know what to look for
and exactly where to go…

Take your time and don't worry about getting lost.
You'll find me.
Up there, a finger and two dots away.

If you're wondering if I'll still be able to hold you
…I honestly don't know…

But I do know that I could still fall for
a swish of light that comes barreling
and cascading towards me.
It will resemble your sweet definite hands.
The universe will bend.
The planets will bow,
and I will say,
"Oh, there you are.
I have been waiting for you. Now we can go."
And the two pilot lights go zooooooooom
into the black construction paper night
as somewhere else
two other lovers lie down on their backs and say,
"What the hell was that?"

CURSING JEFF BUCKLEY

"I couldn't wait for the nightmare
to suck me in and pull me under, pull me under."

SO REAL, from the album Grace
J. Buckley, three years before his drowning

You sultry poison.
You angeldust donor.
You American gunmetal tongue
stealing the power from women.
You said the nightmare sucked you in
and pulled you under.
The muck of the river filling your wide shark-toothed mouth.
You cried out into the hard Southern night
and the moon is still helpless.
You held your breath
and went down.
Young body convulsing in the brackish water
shaking for life,
moaning for the surface June bugs.
Bubbles roared from your throat
filled with swirling notes of terror—
The last melody—the most beautiful.
You said the nightmare sucked you in
and pulled you under.

You died brilliantly.
…but how did you know?

PUSSYCAT INTERSTELLAR NAKED HOTROD MOFO LADYBUG LUSTBLASTER!

pussycat interstellar naked etc etc.
how silly i get.
how lost and silly i get
unravelling my fingers
to where your arms connect.
i come to your body as a tourist.
endless rolls of black and wine film in my fingertips
documenting the places that change your breathing
when touched with the patience of glaciers retreating drip by drip.
it reverses your breath back into the places
that trigger subtle curls in your purple painted toes.
the breaths are not worth hundreds of sparrows,
they are worth all the gray air sparrows die and wander in.
there are things about you i collect and sell to no one.
i journal them in a book you gave me with the inscription,
'don't leave your ribcage in the icicle air. something will break.'
i wrote about the courage my hand would need
aiming down the worn comfort of your hair,
hang-gliding across the summer slits of your winter dress,
searching the perfection in your rock-and-roll breasts,
stealing the heat off the drug of your stomach.
let me die a White Fang death
trembling on the snow and linen of your shoulder blades.

I want to buy you a black car
in 66 shades of black
to match the wandering walls of your heart
filled with the mysteries of space and murder in space.
let me spend my days on the shores of abalone cove island
collecting bottles that wash ashore
and burning the messages inside
to fill them with new messages like
"send more coconuts" or
"send more coconuts and wild boar repellant. i'm re-reading lord of the
    flies." or
"wow, I'm actually on an island. please send my five favorite albums.
I've already built a Victrola out of sand and eel poo-poo.
It's the MacGyver in me. this volleyball won't shut up."
I will float the armada of messages towards the atlantic

and wonder if a pale girl in new york spends time at the shore.
I will wonder if she can see the stars i carved our initials into
when I got sick and weightless.
lay in bryant park and look hard into the air.
your last initial isn't up there
for it is worthless to me
since I had dreamed of changing it.
this is the love of mercenaries.
i'd kill an army of sleeping cubans for the rum desires
in the clutch of your tongue.
touche to your lips!
touche to your way!
touche to your ass!
you are an electric chair disguised as a la-z-boy
and I find comfort in you.
my clear bones take shape in the mouth of glassblower with asthma
for there is no perfection in me
but maybe clarity.

crush me with the satisfaction of your black misted, unclocked breath.
I always come back to the secrets and wonder of your breath.
It is something for sparrows to wander in.
it's not that i wait for you,
it's that
my arms are doors i cannot close.

CHEAP RENT

She, a strange landlord,
pointed to her chest and said,
If you lived here
you'd be home by now.
I, the stranger with no deposit,
pointed to my chest and said,
If you lived here
you would have to be
very…tiny.
I think of her smart hips
and the days left before their unhinging.
Our love was redder than
the eyes of McCarthy.
Our love was blacklisted and strong.
Our love was a brawl in the street
with spectacles on.
Eyes of bayonet knives,
Brass-knuckle sex,
crowbar quarrels
and the nunchakus of my mouth
which I tried to use with great aplomb and theatrical flash
but always ended up knocking myself unconscious.
'No, you don't look fat in that dress.
Yes, that sentence does assume you look
fat in some dresses.'
Kapow. Right in the face.

This love remains a tongueless boy
in a basement
that you snuck graham crackers to.
He loved to see the glaze
of your hammer-and-nail-polish.
You kept him alive.
He paid you with a finger every time you arrived:
One to clean your elfish ear.
Then two
to check your pulse.
Then three
to make
an unbreakable Boy Scout oath.

Then four
for karate.
Then five
so you could rest each one
of his loose fingers in between yours
like couples do when they stroll
through shitty carnivals.

When we first met
she told me of the brilliant in Israel
and the erotic vision of the cynic.
I tried to turn her on by talking to her about
skinning animals.
She kept hunting for a metaphor.
I was actually just talking about skinning animals.
Now I can't stop thinking of how our baby would look in a perm
with massive elk for eyebrows,
and then in comes the Tel Aviv
of her mouth on my dirty neck.
Our mouths building a jangly, red swamp
they will call weirdo Louisiana.
This kiss spills her silent resume:

She is the poster child
for the Willy Wonka suicide camp.
Her stomach is a summer full
of black ice-cream-truck hijackings.
Her eyes are highway fatalities
you can't stop staring at.
Her skin is rehab for sandpaper junkies.
She is my landlord,
and she lowers the rent,
points to her chest and says,
"Man, if you lived here
you'd be home by now."

LAST NIGHT IN PARIS

Say bonjour!
Say au revoir!
Say si vous plait,
or the French will hate you.

I assured my well-traveled friend
that in the City of Love
all I needed to speak was the language of love
(which is of course…English)
and they will come around.
They did not come around.
Was it the Austin bats in my jaw?
The Brooklyn fuck-you in my stride?
The Long Beach bar breath in my fists?
The South Side in my desire?
The mutt in my blood
that sent the foreign legion scrambling for American poets on the radar?
'Hu hu huuuh. Les are ruining everyzing.
Les american poets are stealing all our mademoiselles,
pumping them with their inspiration, and now France is
full of ugly babies with crazy nipples.
What do you do with a silver dollar nipppple!'

We will bleed all over this town
and make you think Hemingway blew his
brains out
because he had to live here for a little bit.

We plant a flag here tonight and this-here Franceland is ours.
All you have to do is plant a flag these days.
That's why we got the whole moon and all you got is Tahiti.

Fine. Walk around all day like you just blew the Devil
and he didn't warn you when he came Hot Tamales.
You are not the city of light or love. I undeclare you.
I am the city of love,
and we executed the mayor years ago. With moonpies!

Eat a bag. Frenchies
Paris,
I bring you a thousand boomboxes in my knuckles.
I bring you bad capitalism in the beginning of my name.
I bring you everything wrong about America
which tonight is inherently right.
A brigade of working class light
charging through your pretense.
We will walk like the boss.
We will love like janitors.
We will drink like we were just laid off.
Tourist boats pass.
Bordeaux goes down.
We yell out,
'Bonjour you fuckin' Frenchies,
Here's to Scotland'…just to throw 'em off.

Au revoir.
No si vous plait.
Voices in the night.
Three cans of graffiti.
You know the colors.
You know where the stars go.

DUMBER FLAGS (SECRET TRACK)

DONT GIVE UP THE SHIP
GIVE UP THE SHIP SOMETIMES

DON'T TREAD ON ME
DON'T TREAD ON ME UNLESS IT'S A THAI MASSAGE

LIVE FREE OR DIE
LIVE FREE AND EAT SHIT AND DIE

COME AND TAKE IT
COME AND TAKE IT, MY STORAGE UNIT IS
A HELL-HOLE

REMEMBER THE ALAMO
REMEMBER THE ALAMO IS WHERE OZZY PISSED
REMEMBER THE ALAMO BUT NOT TO THE OBSESSIVE
    DEGREE OF PHIL COLLINS
REMEMBER THE ALAMO WAS FULL OF BRATS!

GIVE ME LIBERTY OR GIVE ME DEATH
GIVE ME LIBERTY OR BOSS ME AROUND, DADDY

AMAZING JIM

I'm 23. She's 25.
When you lay on your back, your voice sounds different.
I feel like a cloud.
Oh. I've made a woman giddy. Talkative. Abierto.
She used to get her hairspray confused with her deodorant.
How supermarket-hygiene-aisle-Braziliant her locks would smell
And how salon-style-sticky her clean American armpits would feel.
I hear her worlds like a toddler
with floaties
bobbling in blue illuminated night pool.
Sticky…
Uncomfortable but still…
I could never…
Horse glue…
Clumsiest bike…
Something about how she could never do this trick
where you throw your kickstand down as you roll to a stop.
She said she fell like a heavy pancake,
like Jenga in slow-mo.
Lips movin' arms goin' throwin' her kickstand down.
At this point I think of a slow hollow sound.
I didn't bring all this home.
Those pop metaphors.
Those Aquanet armpits.
Those kickstand fingers flicking my chest.

I lay inches from beautiful bedhead
Moonshining hair
500,000 filaments burning.
I cannot cuddle with someone's history.
It takes the anonymity away.
Like hearing a magician's real name.
Like seeing a clown without make-up.
Like honest touch.
How can you hold that.
How could these skinny arms hold all that?
All her clumsy history is kicking my ass.
She pinches my elbow skin.
She says, Amazing. There's no nerves there.
I say, Amazing, I can't feel a thing.

What is the name of that perfect nerve
that tells your eyes to shut tight when pain approaches?
Jim.
Amazing Jim, the magician.
Eyes synchronize shut and now I am no longer here.
No longer bobbling and floating.
Steady. Running.
Running alongside her.
Slowing her down by gripping the back of the banana seat.
Throw your kickstand down… now!
And we fall.
We fall together
Over the spokes
And I feel the spokes.
I feel 'em.
And for as long as they remain shut
I am seven and she is nine.
I feel like a cloud, she says.

And I know this is true,
for I know the terrible things that go on inside of clouds.
That night drags its nails down the wall
and its sounds like…

I Love You Is Back

ALL DISTORTION, ALL THE TIME

Someone plug my lungs back into the guitar amps!
I want to live
on all distortion, all the time.

More over-drive!
Aren't you sick of being appraised as just wholesale?
Aren't you sick of sailing on listing ships?
Aren't you weary from playing cellos with ex-lover's bones?

I want the stomach butterfly brigade to exit this controlled scream.
I want a piano that will not warp outdoors
when the rain demands slow dancing.

I want to skew the difference between Tai Chi and Chai tea,
and end up drinking a tall glass of your graceful force.

I want to lick my hands after I touch someone that has just become
razzle dazzled by the huh?

I want birds to come close enough to hear them speak Aviation Spanish.
Abierto, abierto.

I want your criminal record collection in my throat,
and my thumb in the electric ass of this all night jukebox.

I want my shoulder blades mounted
in the museum of the most fantastic knives.

I want church in a bar and a bar in every church.
I want to pass out and hear you say Amen with your body.

I want a skeleton night light in the closet.
I want your wow in my now so we become NWOW.

I want free shit to not cost anything.
I want to feel like a disco ball of fish hooks
so you can hang on my words, how we spin in small miracles of light.

I want my kitchen to be a Brazilian dance floor
with a pot of your sweat in the oven
and a fridge stocked with booty lust.
I want new sheets. Everyday.
I want your silver muscles cut into a quilt.
Let me sleep under your strength.
I want more pony lamps. No reason. Just give me the lamps.
I want to sing this into all tail pipes until I'm exhausted of puns.

I want to smell the everything.
I want to remember that the sky is so gorgeously large,
I feel stranded beneath it.
When I gasp beneath it,
I only want to gasp
for more.

MY FIRST CPR CLASS

We met at a CPR class for singles.
We learned that the inhalation phase of breathing
is called inspiration.
She said, "If you breathe into someone
else, it should be called something
more magical." I said, "Like expiration?"
She said, "Something more spiritual."
I said, "Resperado!"
We met at a CPR class for singles.
We both showed up early for the poison healing chapter.
During drills, I volunteered to choke.
She volunteered to Heimlich me.
Her tense arms reached around me
like a semi-heterosexual cowboy, pulling hard.
I coughed out a Tic-Tac from the day before and told her it was a tooth.
She said, "Your teeth smell minty."
I said, "That's the nicest thing a non-dentist has ever said to me."
We met at a CPR class for singles.
She was all dressed up in blue emergency.
Styled in the symptoms of shock.
I wanted to tell her some poetic madness,
a vagina wrangling phrase like:
"You are a swinging peppermint nightstick of pink,
crashed on all my horny bionics. I want your hot shampoo
and wet blood now."
All that came out was,
"Hey, isn't it funny how old people really love pie?"
She said, "Isn't it beautiful how old people respect every breath.
We breathe 17 times per minute."
I said, "Less if sleeping."
She said, "Less if kissing."
I said, "And um, or… snorkeling?"

We practiced mouth-to-mouth on the dummy.
She said she was used to making out with guys this tan.
She dropped her gum in its mouth as a joke…for me to find.
I had a hard time retrieving it with my tongue.
I got it after five minutes.
The instructor suspended me from further oral interactions
with all plastic devices within the room.

When it came time for a live volunteer to mimic
an unconscious stroke victim, I beat her to it. I laid down.
She stepped up and I closed my eyes.
I liked her mouth, docking upon mine in its Armenian grip.
I felt upon my lips,
her light moustache that said
"I might look like a cop in
five years."
I knew we had something in common,
and that something was mouth justice.
Later, I moved her lazy lips toward mine and said "I'm always dying."
We kissed like Europeans who just discovered that it's for the best to put
    ice in
a coke.
She breathed into my mouth like a space heater.
Her new gum fell into my throat
and I actually choked.
The instructor thought I was getting into the drill again
and kept the class coming to me, on the table.
A dude with a beard made of tuna fish breathed into me
like a diesel leaf blower.
A nineteen-year-old girl with a goiter and no upper lip
breathe-sneezed into me, wetter than a whale porno.
Then a short, spandexed man who looked like an old baby
slobbered into my tonsils until he pressed his burnt tube steak fingers
into my chest and the Big League Chew rocketed out like a geyser.
We met at a CPR class for singles.
I learned that a mouth finding another mouth
in its desperate gaping,
could land and surrender to shared air,
and the thing that passes between mouths as the lips connect
could save your life.
…that and massive pumping on the breasts.

RECORDING TEXTBOOKS FOR THE BLIND

I had never gone inside the blind man's house before.
I had read his graduate text books

on Astronomy, Polynesian music theory
and strange mathematics into a tape recorder.

All mumbled for him for five bucks an hour in Flagstaff.
I thought it would be nice to work from home and help someone.
It dragged on me.

After two hours of recording
I would begin skipping things that seemed unimportant…to me.
I also added jokes about various pictures in the book.

"And this is a picture of a naked lady with an abacus. What's that doing in here, and when did scientific calculators get that big?"
I never told him that I skipped some stuff.

He couriered a message to me to bring a 40 watt light bulb
and that I would be reimbursed
during my next tape delivery.

When I arrived he asked me to
 help him replace it
so he wouldn't get shocked.

After a few seconds,
I wondered why I was replacing a light bulb in his house.
He said he could tell a difference.

The place seemed cozy and well decorated.

I asked him if it felt like home.
He said nowhere felt like home.

I asked him the most pedestrian of questions, "What's it like?"
"Oh, living alone?"
It's not what I meant but I listened.

He said when you are alone you drink slower.
He said he had a bottle made of bone and how different it felt on his lips
compared to ceramic.
He says when he speaks now, more often he means what he says.

Of course, I wanted to know about living with blindness.
I wanted to tell him I wrote a story about a time
when I was an Easter bunny for some blind kids,
as if that would make us feel bonded.
He mentioned that all he has ever learned about stars rolling in gas,
the sound of Hawaii
and various algorithms
come to his brain as my voice.
He said I was in his head and that when I spoke,
he expected a load of random
information.

I kept moving my hand near him, gently.

I kept trying to tell if he could tell that I was looking at him.
Standing there at his door I tried to tell him
how cold I was because I wasn't wearing a jacket.
I must've sounded nervous.
His record player was dusty.
I didn't know if I should tell him.
I asked him one night,
dropping off the cassette, what he dreamt about.
He said each word crisply:
"Shapes.
Mostly shapes.
And a woman.
How are the light bulbs doing?"

DEBBIE

Attached to a little red plane,
A sky banner floats
above.
DEBBIE, DO YOU LOVE ME?
Not, Debbie, I love you.
Not, Debbie, will you marry me?
It detached from the back of the little red plane,
The sky banner whisping down the sky.
I wondered who it would land on.
I imagine that person having a hell of a day
if their name happens to also be
Debbie. I could see it
making her believe in God.

LISTING MY CONFLICTS

It's OK to be nothing to everyone else
if you are everything to someone else,
especially when everyone you know keeps treating the little nothings
like it was everything.
I am from everywhere I've been
and everywhere else feels like nowhere
when you are where
I am not.
There are a million living poets better than I,
but I have a million poets living inside.
What to feed them!
If Jesus is God then he actually said this,
"I am the way, the truth and the life. No man comes to me except
    through me.
Dear me, take this cup from me."
I have been that vain.
I could use some religion that is in no way religious.
I like the quiet but I wasn't born quiet, I was born screaming.
The older and deafer I get, the more I
need the screaming.

WOMAN SLEEPING IN A ROOM FULL OF HUMMINGBIRDS

Teased by success.
We're like vampires in a tampon factory.

The only good monologue has mistakes.
Mistakes make honey interesting.
Silly putty, ice cream cones and chocolate chip cookies
are all accidents. Me too!

This is a self-portrait of mumbo jumbo.
I drew myself as a Bengal Tiger smacked up out of its orange.
Pacing, just pacing until my next meal.
Hushing my legs out to the twilight poison.
That means nothing! I'm spread.

I was plowing anything
that smelled disinfected and didn't wear pookah shells.
I started making lists to get the stripes back on the tiger.
I was watching my stripes slip from my spine,
laying there on the ground like a bunch of parentheses.

Go away therapy. Flush home pills. Make lists.
My lists started out strange.
#1. Do something rebellious to get out of your comfort zone. Try graffiti.
My first graffiti art said, "Don't pierce your babies' ears.
They don't like it and no one thinks it's cute except for you
and your friends with jet skis." This was coming from me, the only boy
who enjoyed getting circumcised.
#2. Write something down that is impossible and write it as possible.
It took me awhile but I came up with this little gem.

"Be on time. Ride time like a suede cowgirl. Break it.
Make it sack out, then canter. Trim its hooves.
Run it into the ground. Oh no.
You just wrote about time! You are one of
thooooose horrible people. Get to church!"

There was a whole bunch I made, which are a bit embarrassing,
but the last one became my favorite.

#46. One day, when you are tired of being broken
and in the city,
carefully strap little LED lights to hummingbirds,
at least 52 of them
and release the birds in your lover's bedroom at night.
When he or she asks what is going on
tell them to be still,
lay there all broken and impressed.

Watch her mouth move,
astounded at your invention, alow budget meteor shower.
Watch how it turns your lover young
with each awe of shooting light.
See your lover as eternal. Do not kiss them.
Wish your burdens upon those birds.
The birds can take it.
Go play.

THE PROFESSIONAL DRINKERS OF CALGARY, CANADA

I was working in a warehouse in California,
delivering ergonomic floor mats
to people who never looked me in the eyes.

I was alone all day, skateboarding up and down the concrete aisles.
I went on a trip to see somewhere new.
I thought Calgary was so far North, it would fix my head.
It is an easy place to die.
Calgary has a rodeo, private booze holes
and snow mobile parties.
I've settled into a mausoleum of lonely drunks.
They're coming in out of the cold like stiff snow angels
clocking out from working their endless jobs.
Calgary's famed drinking brigade bobs in parade unison
under street lights that fight to shine in sallow air.
Crunch, Crunch, Breath fog. Crunch.

You have to plug in your car in the parking lot to keep it from crumbling.
All shirts tucked deep to the last testicles crinkle.

Frontier blood. Quiet bars.

A young man that walks to the bar from work
talks to me about eating moose,
and how it seemed less humane to eat a moose, the danger.
How can we not love something so big?

The old man in the mustard overalls drinks
like he never wants to go home. What's waiting there?
A mistake?

The TV by the pickles plays the sound of people turning
to the colors of old city snow.
I want someone to talk to me so badly, but I can't.
Why can't I tell them I came from far away?
It kills me. Every day, it kills me that I can't
unstranger myself sometimes. So weird.

THE VICTORY EXPLOSIONS

I try to remember my youth.
It evaporates into 76 memories.
One memory was that you believed
the earth was made perfect by God
and that humans fouled it up
and that sin was something we gave birth to,
as God shook his head at our idiocy.
"How could they choose terror and loss?"
I don't think God really ever wanted perfection
if he designed the things he made with an instinct to screw up.
Fighting it and failing is beautiful and hard.
Screwing up is part of the program. Call it sin. Call it human.
Maybe there are codes built inside of darkness needing light
and vice versa.
It did not shake your belief in the existence of a God,
but it shook your belief in the bland necessity for perfection.
It birthed the belief that the human who could figure out
the balance of a hunger for winning and a deep respect for losing
would win the life trophy.
You go back to the first year you learned to daydream in a clothing rack.
The first year butterflies bloomed adrenalized
in your wet guts.
In the 5th grade, you tempted everything.
Bicycles spinning,
the smell of girls,
pencils at war,
dismantled radios.
Launching off the swing set into the air, your first sensation of flight.
An innocent season for getting your ass kicked by a boy
who thought it would be a nice sign of his love.
Adam White and I liked the same girl.
He heard I'd kissed her underwater at
her Dutch pool party, French
style, which is weird for a 5th grader like me.
I had not even kissed Snoopy.

These were skill sets as a 5th grader; my tongue was not prepared for.
I did not know who started the rumor,
but I was about to pay for it with the cash of my face.
The same field we chased girls together in,

the strong, freckled Adam challenged me to my first fistfight.
I felt like a coward in a costume of a coward.
I was skinnier than a dead model.
No matter how much I denied the rumor,
his freckles kept popping from his face like braille.
"You're ass is grass, Derrick Brown."
I know.
The crowd gathered.
I stared at them like a sparrow trapped in an airport terminal,
wanting sky but stuck against glass.
I stood like a cricket in a junkyard of fiddles
unable to stop my legs from shaking music from my knees.
He swore he loved her, and that I would pay.
His forehead blistering
wrinkling like a crumpled valentine.
Where in the hell were the teachers?
What I wanted was mercy,
but even I didn't know what that word meant.
His fist came out and crushed at my jaw.
My eyes went black and all that I saw
was a shower of lightning bugs.
Children flashing into sunshine.
My teeth penetrating my cheek.
Falling backwards,
blood fertilizing the softball field.
But instead of freezing, I stood up again.
He struck me down, once more.
Eyes, ricocheting against the back of my skull.
The earth, meeting my failure, legs buckling,
skin reeking with contact, and I stood up again.

And he socked me with all his might.
Matchsticks lighting in my cheeks.
And I stood up again.
And he hit me so hard my Mother's eyes bled.
And I fell again, and I stood up again, and again, and again, and again,
until he grew tired of socking me and left. Everyone left.
Alone there, baptized in my own warm blood,
I now knew the cost of the satin sponge and slop of a girl's ridiculous lips.
'Cause guess what?
We did kiss under water at that Dutch pool party
like aqua spies and it was worth it.

There's nothing for me to learn from winning.
It is losing that has yielded the unforgettable lessons.
Losing is pregnant with chance.
Victory escorts loss to every dance.
Harmony,
harmony.

LUCKY IN LOS FELIZ

Los Angeles is a well lit emergency room.

I celebrate the moodfood of Little Dom's and the neon action
of Los Feliz.
LA is a good place to try on clothes that will never be yours.
You're going to run out of money. You're free!
LA is a beautiful cat that doesn't need you. Cats are French.

Each downtown high rise at night is a robots finger
coming out of the silver grave.
She is as understood as expensive silk or images in the airwaves.

On Sunset and Hillhurst there is a bar called Bar Luck.
This bar will be raptured away.

The interior glows in horny reds. Why is red so horny?
Pink can take it or leave it.
Shadows bounce across vinyl booths.
All the leather jackets have been Xeroxed and distributed.
Some poor, poor man has to wear sunglasses inside.

The waitress swallows the loud music into her hair.

There are mirrors on the walls to see who is seeing whom.
I heard a New Yorker talk about how much they hated LA.
I leaned over and told her to stop whining
and that it is wonderful and shitty everywhere, that if you hate LA
you hate the midwest. This place is everywhere.
    Los Feliz is the Paris of LA and it is also a cat.

The truth is that everywhere I haven't been
always seems more wonderful than where I am, when I am broke.

The bartender said to me as I was leaving,
"Are you going to go have fun
somewhere else?" I said, "There's too many people out tonight."
She said, "Thursday is the new Saturday."
I said, "Friday is the new Christmas. Happy Holidays."
She said, "You're lucky. I wish I could go home.
But I gotta make the big bucks."

I said, "I wish you could go home.
I wish you could go to my home
so we can make me peanut butter treats.

Then I would make you think I was going to kiss you but I would
just be looking at your neck tattoos real close."

I left and accidentally walked the wrong way to my car.
To the dim first date kids of Covell. Two wines, where I quiet my heart.
All the way up Hillhurst to the people laying their futures out on the tiny
    tables at Figaro, feeling a softer French resistance
Across the way to see the hot people in dirty clothes spending their last
    dime at Ye Rustic
and then to the quiet thrill of perfect meatloaf and cold beer at Fred's 62
before staring in the window at Skylight at all the books I wish I could
adopt. Someone yelled "Nice shirt, dumbfuck."
He got one of the things right.
Jasmine lifted everywhere and fixed me.

I wonder if there's some metaphor in getting lost
in a town you love,
that doesn't love you back. Maybe I don't need to be loved back.
It's so French. Maybe I need to sit at the bar, in sunglasses, my favorite
shirt, my nice, nice shirt, learning to undo a need for anything.

MY SPEECH TO THE GRADUATING CLASS

You belong everywhere.

The age you are right now is something
you will want back in about ten years.
Be bold now. Tell her you've got a crush.
She won't stab your face. Lose sometimes.

This is the age of exploration.
I ain't talking about Robitussin overdoses
and turning an apple into a bong.
I am talking exploring limits and setting boundaries.
Toilet papering someone's house you love
that doesn't own a revolver.
The parents will forgive you. The cops will forget you.
You are young and that has value. And the value is $29.95.

Get a journal. Document this moment
because the upcoming changes are shocking.
Punks will become political activists in suits,
Hippies will become business people,
Skaters will become graphic designers,
Football stars will become glow in the dark pastors.
Maybe journal it all cause you will forget.

No matter how cool you were at your coolest peak,
in 4 years you will look back at photos and say,
"Lordy I was a big dork."
This will give you the rush of humility.
Be proud of how humble you can be.

College is not a passport to success.
A passport is not a passport to success.
Delaying self-gratification is.
Learn how to not want it now.
If we can save money, organize a game plan,
read, clean up our lives, floss once in a while,
then we will rule the world.

You will forget your locker combos,
the concept of popularity,
and the valedictorian's speech.
You will remember the teachers who cared
and eating Taco Bell like an aardvark without barfing.

You want to be a doctor.
You might end up working at Chili's. At least for a while.
There are jobs out there you don't have to hate.
Pretend it's a game. Pretend you love hardship.
The Crazies have power. Write stuff down.
It feels good to cross things off your list.

It is as hard to forget the bad stuff
as it is to remember the good stuff.
Remember the hallway make-outs. Forget the wedgies.
Most bullies end up on court TV anyway.

Really cool people don't know they are cool.
Some people will try to kick your face in.
Know when to kick back and know when to tell friends
you punched someone's foot with your face.

Young love has about a 20% chance of success.
Try not to get so broken up about it.
Young love is real. So is future love.
Heartbreak makes you funny. Learn what you need.
Kiss with all your might. Then mix it up.

Tell strangers nice things about their eyes or clothes.
You will change their day.
Fire the actors from your life.
Just cause you know someone
doesn't mean you owe them anything.
Especially if they're an energy leech.

Ladies: Tell men exactly what you want.
They are simple creatures. Take him to dinner.

Gentlemen: Tell her how you feel a lot. Listen and ask ask ask.
Notice details about her and say you noticed.
Ask questions and just listen and hold. Plan things.

You always need permission.
You still might get the gift wrong. Try.

If you don't know what you want to be, so what.
You will fall into something. Just do something
or you're just a gassy little speed bump.
Don't worry about being good, just begin.
Fear of starting has ruined so many potential pieces.

Let your parents know you know raising kids is hard.
They may cry. Being alive is expensive
and they wanted you more than fancy romantic vacations.

Always have poor friends or acquaintances.
Desperate friends make the purchasing of luxury automobiles
and useless gadgetry ridiculous when people are desperate.
Somewhere, someone is desperate.

Some people aren't very good at laughing.
They will be mad at you. Wonder how they got that way
and keep laughing. Maybe not in their face.
No one loves a spittle spaz.

Ask old people how they're doing.
The answer will be long.
This will help you slow down.

Go to other countries.
Get into other cultures and talk politics, God and love.
It is the best church.
Meeting other people is the only way to know
if you believe what you believe cause it's been handed to you,
or if it really rings true in your heart.

Getting lost should be seen as a sweet chance to be found.

Remember, you belong everywhere.

THE DEMONS' FIRST DATE

I was so nervous.
I talked about glacial disasters
and owls attacking the gray part of her eyeballs.
They were so lovely, I wanted to hard boil them.

She told me sweetness didn't sit well with her so
she puked into my glass of ox blood. It looked like clams
so we toasted:
"Here's to our brothers in heaven,
may they understand why we exist. To us."

She leaned over hard and kissed my mud black tongue.
Our mouths bashed sparks like the metal salmon
that charge up the river
Styx. So I jammed a fork in her eye.
She went to pierce her poison fingernails
into my chest to pull out my heart
and nibble on it but as she reached into my ribs,
she pulled out…a pet rock,
which is something I usually do at parties.
I had written on it, "look up."

Molotov Cockatiels soared overhead, wings ablaze,
shedding ash, which fell in the shape of cupid's arrow.
As she pulled up her eagle skin dress to defecate on it,
I felt like she could be the one.

I walked her home,
tried to push her down a well
but as she lost her balance, she grabbed my warty hand
and dragged me down the hole with her.
We fell forever.

We landed in hell's sewer, which even for us, was pretty bad.
Crisp onyx crocodiles snapped at our ankles as we kicked lava
puddles at each other.

I pretended like I was going to throw her into their path, until she ran
at them, howling like a pack of stabbed Dobermans.

She ripped their jaws clean from their heads.
She gave two to me and said, "I hope you like book ends."
I felt so... wanted, I cried the realest kitty cat piss.
I didn't even own any books,
except for a controversial one by Salman Rushdie.
The orange clouds drizzled down embers that night
and she held her tongue out.

I touched her fangs and goose bumps ran down her oozing,
imperfect thighs.
"I care for you so much, I'd be willing to be nice for an hour.
Maybe even carry someone's flaming groceries or not hurt children.
I've never said that before."
I really wanted to tell her how much I hated her,
but didn't want to scare her away.
The feeling nagged at me as if the Anti-Christ
was gestating the death of the sun in my abdomen.

I ran my hand across her horns until she fell into a deep sleep,
She awoke and I touched the torch in her esophagus.
Nude, a storm of sledge hammers slid down through the thunder
and I caught one for her and placed it up in her womb,
so she could feel like I was always with her.

I dragged her to a pile of recycled skulls
and beat one into a heart shape and she said, "What is that?"
"It's the human symbol for needing someone."
She bit into it like a Bavarian pretzel and laughed—
another damned kiss and she passed the white pieces into my mouth.
    Communion.

Wolves made of syringes followed us in wonder.
We kicked them in the needles and ran home, knocking over every
newspaper stand, claw in claw,
as warm halcyon splashed the shores of hell's ocean.

HOW THE JELLYFISH WISHES

The farmer's boy was born in a season of drought
and dreamed nightly of the western coastline
where it was rumored that all the stars were migrating
to crash into the sea.
No one knew why this was happening,
but they accepted it.

He awoke with his body in the soft L shape of California
and began to pack.
He was through spending his life between harvesting sweat
and day-gazing upon the scalp of the horizon
for something that felt like home.

He grew up working the soil
and understood that he was like a crop,
that he was just a patch of minerals that rose from the earth
and demanded water and light.
Crops are based in seasons and transformation.
A life, no different.

Corn was a maze his family had been lost in
for generations.
Some years it was beans.
"Everything changes in this farm but us.
Starlight has stopped visiting. I am going West to join it."

He would be the first to seek
the visions, rumored to be streaking light, spittering brightly
into the endless onyx arms of the Pacific.
By dawn, he would not look back.
Orange buckets of light spilled a rusted dusk
across the maple and oaks of Tennessee.

The fields along his route sizzled
with the chamber music of cicadas and bullfrogs.
Possums went squinting at the cackled dawn.
Endless fences poked up like bad teeth in the sunlit mouth
of a fallen giant.
He raced away on a lazy train with eighty dollars crumpled
and a journal.

Lightning had slammed its brights on outside
as he skimmed earlier entries:
"None of the teachers could explain why
the stars were migrating west.
The word on the street was that some states had fell
into a season of mental drought,
where people stopped moving their beds near windows.
They settled into dreaming of bills, tanning salon gift cards
and affordable karate practice.
They stopped wishing.
There was no work for stars here."

When he reached the sea he found headlines in the L.A. Times
stating a theory that the stars had come to light the sea. To reveal.
It was true.
The stars bolted down the highways of nightsky and steam-burst
into the waves. Glowing their metal and rock into cannonball breaches.
They looked like lighthouses being flung into the deep.

How do we know this came to pass? You could see it all.
Have you heard of fish that wish for wings near Avalon harbor?
You can watch them lift into aerials like fat finches.
Have you heard of diatoms that wish for their remains not to be scattered
but to be used in dynamite and toothpaste? The gardens!

The jellyfish wish their hearts to become luminescent.
Some bland fish wish for only the skin of a rainbow.
Have you heard of the humpbacks who wish for the ability to sing for 10
hours straight to serenade their families
swimming back home to the sound
of their voice? Tiny creatures, tired of their fins, asking to become horses
of the sea and they got it. They all got it because they asked.
Because they don't know what silly is.

And who among us has not wished for the sky
to come and show us something?
And how many are waiting and wishing into that sky for relief?
The farmer's boy always wished he could sing.
He dove in.
You could see him underwater.
You could see everything around him.

IN DEFENSE OF SLEEP CONTROL
for JB

All hail the rise of the Chest Tenderizer,
Invisible Friend of the Swallows,
Night Primer, Reverence Combustor,
Horror Choke.

How lucky I am to live this day
far from the lazy noose of the Tennessee Moon,
far from the cold hiss and clacking masts of Nowhere Bay,
far from the Carolina buzz of bullets and foxhole pestilence,
close to the thin arms of you.

Your engine cooing, purr-purr of deep rest.
The coiled lover, defending herself in sleep.
You are this dream of transparent blouses.
We watch our lovers in this state, speaking words into their hair
to shape the mares. To load their days with impulses
and notions they will feel as their own.

I whisper:
You came as vibrant Aster,
drunk lamp lighter, igniting wild the fences.
Kiss cloaker, sexually crippling, shin shattering beast of gladness.
A full flask for a death bed.
Unable to un-gorgeous or disrobe your symmetry.

May your morning lips volley their rain and saffron down upon my tin
    thin skull.
May your legs outsoft the others.
How you rest like a love among brothers.
So lay long as I breathe upon you these small songs.

I exhale across your neck so you may find your nightmare maze
breezed open through the tall fields of the now bowing wheat.
I will cover you with the down
and you will feel the sun warm through
the Godless tundra of your second dream.

I will kiss your shoulder
and the vultures in your slumber

are chased by millions of smaller birds
scrambled into a bazaar of flight.
So many birds, with yellow eyes,
above becomes a starlit night.

I whisper:
Dawn Primer, Daylily Combustor, Horror Choke.
Gloom Tenderizer, Invisible Friend of the Swallows.
Let me in. Let me in.

SCANDALABRA

COTTON IN THE AIR

Your polished back is arched like Saint Louis.
Uh.
I can see your fingers pushing into the bricks
when I lift your hair
to smell October drain from your neck.

You are cotton caught in the air;
I am unfurling all the laces in your body.
I move on you steady like a fleet of ships pushing ice.
I want to break it all.

Your tank top strap slips down the huh huh of your shoulder
and I will not strain meaning from this.
I am waltzing a wrecking ball and I know it
and I love it.

I am wading in the dark felt Tijuana paintings of your hair.
I am molting my bed clothes uncoiling towards Sahara.

All I want to do is hot lust you into dead sweat.
To watch your legs, those bent sickles,
to watch them shake
like poisoned wrens.

I am gnashed and dazzled.
Smother me in the exhausted thrust of your yes…
wet
as all exploding laundromats.

May I be the image you turn to
when you are heaving alone,
burning like Halloween in Detroit?
I am breathing up your legsss—spitting at the hiding nightingale.
Drift your breasts into my mouth
and I will be that doped up, spinning victrola.
La la la la la la.

I want to make love to you while you're wearing figure skates
until the hardwood floors are toothpicks.

I want to kiss your throat in a dressing room with my hands
bound around your voice.
I want you to leave your boots on in your apartment
so we march our bodies across the ceiling
and confuse the neighbors.

I don't care if you made that dress,
I will shred it until you look deserted.
You're as restless as a New Orleans graveyard in a storm
with the coffins boiling up to the surface.
That's all this writing is. You are across from me and the
soup is cooking.

I sit up all night listening to your dental records.
I will teach you of exorcism and screw the hell out of you.
I will carry your steam in my mouth.
Daydreaming of the evening of loud struggle.
Call my name—I will cascade like a suicide.
I will fall upon you like a box of fluorescent bulbs
dropped from a five-story building.
I will do anything you ask...
unless I have been drinking; then it is opposite day.

I can't believe you can sleep through all this.
Chunks of brick in your fingernails.
Mortar on your pillow.
A bomb shelter
sketched on your skirt.
Safe.

VAGUE SUBJECT MATTER

Every morning she wakes up after me.
The dawn yawning through the windows.
I watch her sleep.
I sometimes kiss her arm and she just slings it up over her head
as if a mosquito was seducing her.

She sleeps like a sunken fishing vessel.
I put my ear to her chest and there are brittle wind chimes
and the sound of diving boards.
In the evening, after TV dinners and beer,
before we lay down, there is some talking over our books.

"Is everything going to be all right?"
she mumbles before drifting off.
I always say no and kiss her on the forehead.

I bought a pair of shoes with some color in the sneakers.
I ain't so dark, babe.
She can't get it on unless she has tea and toast first.
I sometimes sing while making her tea and toast.

I hum and she sleeps through the work alarm.
I lay on top of her.

She says, "Ahhhh. Man weight."
It's time to get up, darlin'.
"But I don't wanna go to... church."

I love how she dresses like a bowl of flowers in a dive bar.
I like listening to her bare feet hurry around, clumsy scutter.
She calls me a dirty word and it means she loves me.
I kiss her and squeeze the avocado breast.

I can see those scenes still.
Now that she is gone, all poems shorten.
I wonder if I can sell a bed so big,
so full
of so many types of mornings.

VALENTINE'S DAY IN DRESDEN

I feel as ridiculous as faith-based food,
directionless like rain in outer space
when you reach for me.

Don't unfurl your vanilla fantastic at my black molasses.
Our love would be as dumb
as a bomb on a boomerang.
You are sacred, ugly solace
and sweet enough to have dentists boycott you.
Figs in your lips.

Let's not fall in love.
I am tired of stroking that kitty.
I am tired of the colon cancer
from the smoke it blew up my porthole.

Don't show me that you are
an observatory of wet hot bummers and boy germs.
Don't come to me all dressed up in a peanut butter and
nightmare sandwich.
Your eyes as boring as a desert photograph,
your body, a nude model for bad hotel art.

Jealous as a lush,
I know you will apologize in the morning for all the
misplaced I love you's.

I know your type. I know your font. Wingdings!
Zapf Dingbats! Verdana... wide!
You're a European mess
rolling around in my favorite dress,
a mouth full of hell
and a chest full of hell yes.

Big deal, your eyes are green and gray.
Shut off the night vision, ya creep.
You say you can see halos streak down onto the tarmac?
Those are your drunk friends,
former guardians illuminating the dark interstate.

I know that you hope love will come and get you
but it might rise up and banana split you,
so knock it off with the eyes, sister.
You kissed me on the throat.
What is wrong with you?!
That's where I make my money!

You made my heart go Max Roach.
The rude noise.
Our sex is just going to be a constant bungled stumbling
into each other's gross.
It is going to be like throwing pasta against the wall
to see if we're done.

I know your favorite drink is casual tea.
Don't pour it on me.

Get me to the hospital, now!
I'll have to tell the doctors how good I was feeling that day
and beg them to operate
to get me back to poetry normal.

Speak love all you want.
I don't believe what you say
but
I appreciate your tone.

MEATLOAF

My mother is washing the dishes and singing
a song about someone dancing on the moon.
She stops to pat the globe of her stomach.
"So full."

I help her with the dirty meatloaf dishes and pass them
from the table.
The gunk slides through the soap
and the green goo slips across her strong hands.
There is a flash of light every time she turns
her palm through the soap.

My mother has a small diamond
that she received on her wedding day.
It was given to her by my father,
as a symbol.
It was very affordable.
I always asked her why a diamond meant
that you loved someone?

Why not a brick, snail, wombat, or cat brain?
Why not give someone a pair of handcuffs
to show the world that this person will be with you forever?
Why not a steamroller
and you can tell your love that your world is flat without them?
Why not give them a trophy full of zombie lipstick to
prove that you will kiss their brains out?

There is dishwashing liquid in a brigade of bulging bubbles
and the "tink spink" of moving plates, and my mother is singing
again.
To her, that diamond ring is a cheap, special reminder:
The filthy forks sift through her hands as the disposal burls:
"Gnrlwygnlrygnlrywy."

She stops singing and turns off the disposal.
Her face turns the color of the kitchen sink walls.
Water off.
She tosses through the plates.
She pulls out a rubber doo-dad to check the garbage disposal,

continues frantic, shivering desperate and reaching for ten
minutes.

I wait for her to say it.
I can feel my face, ready to burst like a cloud.
"It's gone. I can't believe we were just talking about it and
it's gone."

She pats my head and hands me a paper towel.
"It's okay, Mom. It's just a thing."
"Not really." She starts to weep a little. "Excuse me."

She goes to the bathroom to blow her nose,
returning, kissing my head and going back to washing the
dishes with me,
scanning every bubble's gleam for the rock.
I roll my damp paper towel into a ring and give it to her.
"If we weren't blood, I'd marry you. And I'd stick around."

She replies, "That is sweet. Illegal, a little weird, but so
sweet, Derrick."
She grabs some tape so it would stay wrapped up.
I sneak outside to the neighbors' place
and steal her a brick
from their garden.

When I come back in,
she smiles and begins to sing that song
of someone somewhere
dancing on the moon,
a song about a boy spinning in the dark
with a beam of light.

CHURCH OF THE BROKEN AXE HANDLE

Lord, my friend's heart has disassembled.
So broken, it is red dust.
His pen is rust.
His body is not a house built for silent prayer.

It is a church of blood, raw and razor pumping
for that scar power, axe handle snap and dirt face gospel.
We belong to the same church.
Our clergy: blacksmiths and cut throats,
former party murderers
and never again to be bound choir.

Our lobby holds a bowl of holy water
filled with terrified jellyfish.
Come wash your hands in it again.
Feel the frenzied sting of his creatures.
It is the Lord's idea to have the sting.

We are the horror in the Lord's love poem.
He has given birth to us to sing in the fight.
We are the organ full of bees, enemies of silence.

Sing out your death rattle constant.
Sing out your questions with the force and mess of
dynamite stew.
Listen for an answer echoing,
spinning warmth inside you like a Leslie speaker.

You will hear it when you are so alone
you wish someone would come and try to kill you
just to hear what your cries to heaven sounded like
when heaven was listening.
I know you are alone and soaking in it
like solitude is blood
and the night is the letting.

Your heart races
with the pressure
of everyone in the room
finding a slow dance partner but you.

Tap in. Tap the shoulder.
Love is yours.
Make the first move.
Lose the ones who stepped on your shoes.
Love is yours.

Let it be its horrible self. Learn it.
Our church is fully armed. Return to it with devotion.
Your spirit is a ready gun. Load it yourself.
Only fire it into the worthy.

Rise above the grief bait and sugars of sorrow.
Spin searing gold from all that copper noise.
You are better than the demons whispering in your cheeks.
The floors of self-doubt are weak.
Do not fall where the heavy have fallen.

Lift us into your belief, let it blast.
Let it be a bloodbath
with your innards on the floor,
no apologies.

Welcome yourself to ugly glory, you.
This is not typical church.
We will not yell
about sin and hell
for that picture doesn't work anymore
for those who have worked on its factory floors.

We welcome you, you new crawling psalms,
you drunk choirs,
you gouged melodies,
you nasty bags of glowing mercy.

We welcome those with unpaid bone tariffs,
those raised by the missing,
those boys who got lost in the eyes of another boy,
those who loved the cities that hated them,
those who keep putting on their gloves for boxing the sanity out,

those who couldn't scratch their golden tickets because
their nails
were ground down from clawing their own way out of
their father's casket,
those who couldn't get skinny enough to get to the front
of the line,
those who couldn't stand anymore so they built splints out
of words,
out of their own words.

Depth charges, yes!
The choir charging the audience with tambourines in their
teeth, yes!
Kick me when I'm up, yes!
Hallelujah, we are fucked! Yes!

Bring it on so we can lift ourselves out of the magpie
swamp.
The worst thing you have ever been through is always a
fair fight.
Come to the church of the new.
A building that only says lost and in bold letters, found.

This is not typical church.
This is a low attended funeral,
a skinny sinner bugger kegger,
a piñata full of doves that demands
beautiful release...

Buddy, you are church.
A house of healing that...
is the closest thing to the image of salvation
since people thought to hold hands
when jumping to their deaths from the failure of buildings.

Open the gates, my friend. Send St. Peter home.
All are welcome.
Turn on the golden lights.
Guide us in.
Someone you have been waiting for is coming.

Guard your heart minimally. Security threat, beige.

You can carry a knife and still trust everyone.
Carry it in your mouth.
Every time you open it,
we await the sharpening noise of worship.

Cry out into the darkness
the sermon that doesn't cease:
You cannot be abandoned.
You can only be released.

PATIENCE

I can not love you until you can love our beautiful waitress
in the simple way that I do.

GROCERY LIST

Be more forgiving.
Substitute "goodbye" for "I like your face."
Spend two nights a week not drinking to forget.
Listen to your body.
Listen to someone else's body.
Get limber.
Don't dog yourself to feel humble. It never works.
Lift others up onto your back until you are sore.
Write for yourself a movie that doesn't end.
Eat a churro slowly.
Kiss your mother on the cheek and don't miss.
Remember that now is barely now. It will soon be back then. Stop.
Don't text anyone while talking with anyone.
It will morph you into a total Butthole.
Finish everything.
Get Milk.

FULL METAL NECKLACES 3
for andrea gibson

I just wish you were here again to talk fast.
I just wish you were in the kitchen dancing weird.
I just wish you could see how everyone feels about your love.

You came to me days after and what a mind fuck that was.
I woke up crying.
I stood at a gazebo by a pond and you said, *Hey. I'm here.*
Your arm around me. You said, *It's okay. It's totally okay.*
I started crying in the dream and woke crying.

Of you course it is you that is the one to give me some
woo woo shit
when I pushed so hard against it for so long.

Thank you.

I almost got a tattoo of the last thing you ever said
I fucking loved my life

But Im waiting for you to come back and choose the font.

TOP

A soldier once told me,
"Killing kills your sense of seeing the living as sacred.
Once you get that out of the way, you're not afraid to die out here alone."

Master Sergeant JC and I write back and forth.
We went to the same basic training, Airborne school
and were stationed in the same Airborne battery.
I got out from the 82nd and he stayed in to run the whole battalion,
fifteen years later. A huge, buff man with a laugh like a side of beef.

He is now guarding Highway 8 in Baghdad.
He has been advancing rapidly in the ranks.
I used to call him Sarge,
then Smoke,
now Top.

He told me about a meeting with his younger sergeants
after the troops had been walking through Kut
and getting pot shots at them.
The Sergeants told him it was slaughter
to go in there without armored personnel carriers.
He relayed this info to get gear before the patrols
and the Captain relayed his orders back:
Patrols in Kut must continue on foot according to Centcom.

I started to ramble about the frustrations of military inefficiency.
There is a difference between talking to someone about war
and talking to someone in war about it.
"Don't do it, Derrick."
Do what?
"Don't make me feel like we're dying for nothing."
I won't. You aren't. They aren't.
"We are freeing these people."
Right.
"If we didn't do it, no one would've."
I know...
"I miss my wife, Derrick."
I talked to her. Cindy is good. The dogs are good.

"I miss Sam Adams beer."
Can't help ya there.
"We are getting picked off. We are wondering when can
we fire at will
and have the soft targets off the list
and engage the enemy in
Mosques, all that."
Soon.

Where am I, John?
Cannoneer #2, round loader, breech puller,
foxhole digger, non-rigger, fuse counter,
aiming pole runner, M60-toting,
ambush crushing grenadier, Specialist Brown is now
just a writer and I am proud of you.
I want you to remember home.

The bars are full of laughter.
The ribs are falling off the bone.
Summer is coming.
You can golf in the twilight.
I want you to miss these things.

I don't care who wins.
I want you to stay alive.
Keep your weapon clean.
Stay alert.
Stay alive.
Kill everything.
Fight everything.
Just stay alive, John.
Keep yourself alive.
There are prayers in your boots.
March.
Come home awake.

I will tell you a story.
This is the job of poets.
Staying alive is the job of good soldiers.
And the dead are better soldiers.
This is not how the world needs you,
or anyone.

The world doesn't need any more sudden dead.

Even though you're good at it,
war
is just one side losing less.

THE LONG, OUTSTANDING SALTATION INTO WILD OPEN AIR

Oklahoma City, Oklahoma
I stopped at Galileo's bar in the Paseo district.
Free beer if you are featuring your poems. Of course I did..
Someone tried to sell me dirty DVDs in the parking lot.
One was called ass ass ass
when the title triple ass would have done just fine.

He didn't want to trade a poetry book for the movie.
Poetry will be worth more than lo-fi fake lust soon.
I remember making out once with a woman
in a handicap elevator around here.
Rowdy stumble-touch
is better than classy balance.

The night air here is flat.
The day is crème and crimson.
I know Dylan Thomas left a beer can onstage when he spoke at OU.
It was on display for years.
Someone stole that empty beer can.
Did they put it up to their ears like a seashell?
Middle American exit noise and dust bowl wrath poems.
Not worth more than
hand streaks
all over an elevator wall.

Norman, Oklahoma
My friends Beau and Jody are getting married today.
I got ordained online and agreed to pastor their wedding
in the middle
of this cross country tour.
He has a lumberjack's beard and a strong Springsteen half-sober face like a gunstock.
She has a white tinsel smile and jar of black olives for hair.
The ceremony was loose and real.
An older woman and I talked about how jealous the non-talking snakes
in the bible must have been of the Lucifer snake
and the first true love, *whatever that is*.

I danced with Beau's sister and threw her everywhere
as "Purple Rain" was ripped open by good guitar
drunkards.
I remember a father, slow dancing earlier with his
daughter. Clumsy, gentle and unashamed.
He held her like he would miss her terribly.
When he let her go,
it was true and perfect.

Tulsa, Oklahoma
The moms here sure are attractive.

Portland, Oregon
I made love to a wonderful woman, urgently
on a sidewalk holding onto a tree at night, in a neighborhood.
She said, what if a car comes?
I said, then that car is a pervert.

Shoshoni, Wyoming
Pass the mellow hush of Powell
and all the curving river gorges of Thermopolis
to get to Shoshoni. The town is a sad song.
Don't you love them?

The Silver Sage bar smelled like stuffed raccoons and mop water.
The waitress told us they were closed.
She was as kind and as busy
as you could be in a town full of white dust and broken glass.

Across the street of abandoned shops,
someone spray painted a poem next to a drawing of Geronimo.
Beautiful words
and no one to read them.

Boulder, Colorado
Everyone here looks like a fitness coach on wippets. The air crunches
like snow that isn't cold.
Some people shouldn't die.

Denver, Colorado
The Mercury Café is a chocolate éclair, dark, sweet and full
of weird goo.
At some point during the show, I threw some chairs to get
at an audience member texting during my set.
Unhinged is a terrible way to sell books.
There sure are a lot of folks here with face piercings.
They look like fish
that fought hard
and broke away from the line. Proud of you.

Omaha, Nebraska
It says the good life,
but it is flat as fuck.
You don't have to have beautiful
surroundings
to be surrounded by beauty. Good music here.

Chicago, Illinois
Their bones are bright
and full with freezer burn.
The bicycles are drunk.
The lips of Chicago wrap around me in sausage skin.
The city is a heaving castle with asthma, rising from a lake
that doesn't end.
Shoulders full of concrete and black ice, lift me up, lift me up.
Heaven's pub. Speak easy to me.
You laugh so hard in Chicago
your ribs rip and it feels like you're kissing
a dark-haired woman
in an elevator full of beetles.
Best people in the whole damn world.
18 degrees and still barbequing.

Dayton, Ohio
Everyone gets lost in Ohio.
I dropped my virginity around here at 19 and
it reminds me that I want to tell my friend
who has a broken heart,
"Don't ruin love
by wanting it so bad."

Traverse City, Michigan
Come see the opera house dance floor where I split my pants
at the world's most gorgeous place for a poetry show!
Come see Michael Moore's beautiful theater of cheap popcorn
and starlit ceiling wonder!
Come see the cherries placed into every object known to man!
Come watch the world blossom in a secret code.
Come see the lake as it calls to the lovers
and come see the lovers answer
by walking into it, hand in hand
and never returning.

Providence, Rhode Island
There were so many pretty girls here
I just went to bed.

Bangor, Maine
This isn't right. This just isn't right at all.
Cristin, her room across the hall,
with door open, called me and yelled into my phone
at the Bangor Motor Inn,
"I'm gonna murder you!"
Then she hung up.
I went to call her back,
but her phone was already ringing.
I knew she would answer it and think it was me.
It wasn't. She might have been embarrassed for how she answered
the phone. I soon called her back. I said,
"You're gonna get dead!"
She responded, "That's not right. That's not right at all.
We're all gonna be dead. Try again."

Royalton, Vermont
We showed up to Mongo's ranch house in a tiny van
and we were covered in hot exhaust and cramps.
There was cold beer waiting and it wasn't bug season.
Do you know what that's like?
When you really want beer and it is already waiting for you
like a war bride, all cold and horny?

Jamaica Plain, Massachusetts
There is a little white house aptly named The White House
full of musicians, artists, and writers.
I spent the day at the huge pond, rowing a boat with some friends.
The swans swam in pairs. I slept somewhere alone.

I got a slab of ice cream that blew my mouth to shreds
at JP Licks and I don't even like ice cream. I'm lactose.
I met a woman on the street while I was carrying my laundry.
She was a belly dancer. Weird how that happens.
You got a big burden
of smelly clothes
and someone offers to help you.

We chatted about wine, staying limber and other things I
know little about.
We didn't get it on, but I sure felt good in her place.
The sepia tone show at the white house was in a little
family room.

Perfect, no amp and packed.
There is a bag of chips with a retractable string in the
living room.
You can pull it down from the chandelier
and offer it to someone and as they reach for it, laugh as it zips
back to its home.
I too want someone to tug on me with the smell of ocean
so I can zip back home.

White River Junction, Vermont
This is one of my favorite towns in the world.
It is about as big as a slice of bologna.
Everyone here is bundled up and smart.
I need to open up a bar here.
Maybe it can be a library too.
I can't read when I'm tipsy
but maybe somebody can.

Hanover, New Hampshire
The leaves are changing like teak on a boat.
The students are wishing for warmth and it doesn't come.
The dorms are kissing chambers trembling in brains and
expectations.

There is water when you enter this town
and a bridge that makes you feel like you are flying into
green laundry.
I could live here
if I was allowed to teach
all the words I have been trying to say
all this time.

College Park, Maryland
Kenton, Gabi, Harry,
you are all I know of the good of this city
and you're from everywhere.
The stromboli is as big as your brave-guts.
Write your way back home.

Drinking and talking about the worst things we've ever done.
Julie was kind and too thoughtful to make that game
forgettable.
Heather was gorgeous and doing pushups.
I think she was getting ready for Armageddon,
her arms, sleek as solid snakes.

Nashville, Tennessee
In a drawl,
I missed you. Grimeys!
Say hi to the wonderful Diana Lee Zadlo.
Ask her for a sammich or some magic tricks.

Franklin, Tennessee
There is a garden here
where over a thousand civil war soldiers died
in hand-to-hand combat.
You can touch your fingers to the bullets embedded in the brick.
This is also a town known for having a large population
of contemporary Christian musicians.
So much blood in one spot.

Austin, Texas
There are clearly two lands called Texas.
There is the land of my father, in Cleveland, Humble, and Houston.
It is a land where you could blow up a car
and no one would care.
It is a land where we chased goats
and got chased by hornets and snapping turtles.
It is a hard land to be raised on and I see it in my father's laugh lines.

Then there is Austin.
You can fall in love with someone, but for only four years.
Then, they graduate, leave and it is all understood
suffering.

My father came to Austin to see the show, ragged from the drive from Humble.
A woman was talking to him for too long so he got up
mid-conversation, kissed her on the cheek
and walked to smoke one of his Salem cigarettes.
I thought that was a great way to excuse yourself.

I know he loves people, but maybe he isn't used to them.
I see myself in him as he stands alone at the back of the venue watching me, watching himself.

Amarillo, Texas
There were wild horses.
There was your friend, Kelly Brown, who just had a child.
Amarillo is where wind and babies meet
so the children dress like kites, grow up and usually lift away.

At the Nat Ballroom, you can dance on the same stage that
Buddy Holly got hoarse on. The road never ends.
There is love in the barren.
The horizon is a train in quicksand.
We sold body tackles for a dollar.
This meant I would tackle you for a dollar.
We needed gas money. We were moving on.
Wild horses stomp and my spirit falls in love
with being alone.

Truth or Consequences, New Mexico
Near the Rio Grande, we pulled over at night.
The sky, gashed with stars,
only the high beams of truckers scooting beneath it.
Anis joked that this is what he usually saw during love making.

It was so dark,
he ended up picking up a souvenir rock. He called it his
lucky rock.
I saw that he lifted it from the spot
I peed in when I got out of the van.
I wonder if he kept it?
I wonder if I should tell him?

Hatch, New Mexico
Blood red chilies hung on the doors as year-long wreaths.
It is 93 degrees here on October 26.
We ate at Sparky's BBQ.
Michelle stood behind the counter,
beautiful and far away, moving in the kitchen
like a youth pastor's wife.

It has been the same lemonade recipe for ten years.
The moose above our table seemed to be smiling.
I would like my head mounted with a confused
look on my face, looking back at the person I thought I knew,
now bringing me down for petty cash.

The sausage and ribs are glazed in secrets and butte powder.
The lemonade and you, they are your father's pride, Michelle.
Michelle, please get in the van.
The river is drying up.
The world awaits your sweet illumination.

Tucson, Arizona
There was a train moving behind the stage door,
every 15 minutes.
I wanted to open the backstage door
to just get on and go.
The people in the audience would have never
forgotten that show.

Long Beach, California

Alex's Bar
Joe Josts
Crow's
The Hawk
The Grasshopper

If you can hit all these places in one day
then you win the tournament of champions.

Long Beach, I will be your unknown gutter laureate of 4th Street.
I will sing from the Gondolas of Naples
to the Merchant Marine staring out from Ocean Street.
He is waiting for the brothers who didn't make it to shore.

Long Beach, you are opening your arms.
Bring us your graduated broke, your sheared babes and
floor peanuts,
your booze parade of labor, your renovated bones,
your shipyard ghost war.
You are spectacle in the sea of blue collars,
a gala of people hanging on
in unison.

Reno, Nevada
All you kids
left to rot here
are brighter
than all these casinos
smashed together.

San Rafael, California
We invited the entire audience onto the stage.
We are all the show.

Berkeley, California
Bringing poetry to Berkeley
is like bringing a turkey

Cottage Grove, Oregon
I spent three nights here recording a poetry album,
at Richard Swift's house,
sleeping behind the controls.
I asked the brilliant fuzzy head of Richard
if he knew where he would hang his hat,
his final resting place.

He said "Here, in Cottage Grove. We love it.
So many people come here and don't want to leave.
You start to love the rain."
The rain comes down, slow enough to see it somersault.
The Ax and Fiddle has good beer on tap
waiting for us as we stroll damp and ready for the night.
We sit and I don't say much, except shit talk Ryan Adams.
He's a kind of cool no one needs to talk about.
Rest in peace, Richard.

Bellingham, Washington
It is the last stop before Canada.
We sang songs at breakfast.
We sang songs at The Beaver.
A new president was elected tonight.

People ran through the streets with American flags,
most of them artsy-looking types.
I wonder if all those flags were just waiting in their closets
like their favorite coat,
and everyone
all at once
was overwhelmed
with the welcome feeling
of new snow.

Our Poison Horse

THE STARGAZER IS DYING

And I'm telling you to live, to hang on.
I'll change the low water in your vase.
We can jam you back into the ground.
Spring is in approach.
The squirrels are being photographed.
There is a flood of sunlight coming,
the rivers are rising for swimming.

Why do you give such sweet smells
before going?

This color is all you get to do?

You made the dead house wonder.
You made this gaze bloom.
We carried your beauty to others
and said,
Can you imagine seeing this in the wild?
Can you imagine how beautiful
it would be if it were still alive?

THE RUINED LIFE

Your life is ruined
when one lost person becomes a loved, low song
and you stop searching
for new music, convinced it will all sound the same.

Your life is ruined
when you won't make her dinner
because you hate dirty dishes
more than you love her grateful sigh.

Your life is ruined
when you hoped the violence
you saw in him
would protect you from the world, and how sad that it did.

Your life is ruined
when someone makes you choose
science or miracles
without seeing how well they party.

Your life is ruined
when you realize too late that the magic it takes
to change someone
exhausts all your magic.

Your life is ruined
when all your friends tell you to get married
because it makes buying a house easier,
but you never see them 'cause it demands so much work.

Your life is ruined
when you begin to rebuild your home
before the last bomb falls and the war
is declared over.

Your life is ruined
when you begin to rebuild your home
before the last bomb falls and the war
is declared over.

Your life is ruined
when people holding hands
while riding bikes
just seems dangerous.

300 BONES

Roy Sullivan still holds the record
for being struck by lightning 7 times over the span of 20 years
and surviving. He left this earth by his own hand.
The lightning could not take him down.

I can imagine the first time it found him.
Out in his pickup truck at night,
remembering that a truck can diffuse lightning
but not if the window is down—Vajam!
feeling the first blast of light wash over him fast
like a fire hose gushing electricity, turning him all x-ray,
hands steaming, hair sizzling, heart shock-jacked, hot organs huddled up,
a left hook from the heavens.

The second and third time it struck him
it all felt sudden and ridiculous.
An impossible stroke of luck.
The news trucks showing up.
Mr. Lightning Rod. The Human Conductor. Roy, the Lightning Sucker.
Priests in their hickey hiding collars, using his tale as allegory,
telling kids that God physically punishes the wicked
when we step out of his love.

The fourth and fifth time, people distanced themselves from Roy.
Scared of what ire he draws from the angels
and all the forces of the heavens.
He was gunpowder.
He was a marked target.
His boots flying from his feet.
Laces still tied.

A jug of water to douse his burning hair,
always at the ready in the passenger side.
His wife leaving him after he was struck.
The news turning his magic, common.

The sixth time. No one came.
Roy's fingernails black and gray. A scar down his shin. Hair crisped.
The doctors gave him aloe vera and told him to be careful.
They couldn't explain why he wasn't dead.

Roy moved through the town like a ghost
even when the sun was shining.
No return to normalcy when the world christens you as bad luck.

The seventh time.
Roy noticing thunder clouds rolling towards him,
daring them to speak. "Try and take me. Try and take me away."
A smile welling up in his burnt molars when he feels it start to sprinkle.
It strikes. It bullets down, whips his legs out. He is unconscious.
His suspender buckles, like stoves.
He pulls himself through the mud
to the passenger side of his truck,
dumps the water on his head.

One reporter returned to the emergency room
for a follow up story on Roy's impossible world record:
"7 times, Roy. Aren't you scared that you've pushed your luck?
Most people die from one.
Will you still go outside to work if there's a storm?"
Roy replied in simple southern notes:
"I will still try to."

The reporters asking Roy, "What was it like?"
Roy sitting up and clearing his throat.
"What was it like? It hurt. It all hurt.
The lightning and everything else. Losing friends.
But I'm glad it happened.
I feel strong. I feel strong the way you feel strong from love,
and I see now that I can't go
until I get it all out. I am so full.
I have to get it all out. If God wants it back, he picked the wrong fight.
It's mine.
It has always been mine.
My heart beats on.
My bones are strong.

Five times stronger than steel,
not poetically—scientifically.
We are born with 300 bones, and we die with 206.
This means
there are bone guzzlers in the shadows.
All dressed up in No, thank you's and Get lost's.

They will come for you,
and you must douse them in jars of blood, cum, flowers, yes, color,
fast power, truth stripped, hard loss, tongue kissing, sorrows bazaar,
flight, love, love, love, and 100,000 beats.

Money broke up with me a long time ago.
Do I still live like a shower scene Psycho scream?
I still try to.
I stopped reading the bible
and started believing in miracles—
alive is a miracle.
Your life is medicine to someone.
You gotta go find the sick.

Do I still dance even when all the great dance halls are all closing down?
One dance floor closes down
and the streets open up
and the canals freeze over
and the rooftops get ready
and the backyards of night are lighting up
and the parks are wide and wide open
and the empty bars are turning up the music
and the abandoned buildings, all dressed up like us,
are broken into and lit up like New Year's fireworks in Iceland.

Will you still dance
when no one needs to dance with you?
Lightning is striking somewhere, all the time.
Wait for it to roll the horizon.
Feel your bones ready for the light to burst.
Bones will be all you are.
May your radios be too loud.
May you lose your voice singing the road trip eternal.
May you let it all out.
May you stand fast in the crushing storm when there is no shelter.
May you challenge the heavens.
May you dance on the wreckage after dismantling the myth of constant hell. May you dance the jaws of life.

Great power comes at weird times in the strangest places.
Winston Churchill was born in a woman's bathroom

during a dance.
May you enjoy the courtship
and hail its arrival.
May you make yourself big
when facing the awakened bear of your fears.
May you dance the dance of the unknown.
May you get the hell out.
May your heat melt all the sand
to make us see us.
May your heart move you so wild
your love
scars your legs.

PLACES YOU SHOULD NEVER KISS

1. In a Men's Warehouse, not the suit store. A warehouse where they make lousy men.
2. Conservative foam party. Not right wing conservative, conservative as in the soap is rationed so no one gets too fucky.
3. On the Peter Pan ride at Disneyland. Don't kiss while fake flying. Notice how you move over the darkness. Pay attention to tiny London. Tiny London is paying attention to you!
4. At a gun range after happy hour. Everyone you love is one bad joke away from leaving you for good.
5. In a city that doesn't get its own jokes.
6. Um. Never kiss someone who is searching for a word and tells you they are blanking. They will think you are putting words in their mouth. It's much worse.
7. In front of someone in Malibu with a sense of humor.
8. Inside of a literal white Russian. It must break you.
9. At a vegan BBQ while everyone compares the glisten of their fake meat sweats around the L.E.D. campfire, embracing the future, embracing a lack of joy until that becomes joy. Do not kiss them until they admit they are meat.
10. In a gay western seafood bar called Fish and Chaps.
11. You should never kiss someone who is trying to enjoy a churro. A churro is just a donut with a boner.
12. During a conversation at a party full of comedy improvers, which was to be a positive step in the emotional reconstruction of Derrick Brown, but the improv rule powers every conversation "don't deny." So yes, I WILL have another drink with dumb ass fruit in it; and everyone will yes, wear their church pants into the above ground pool; and yes, you will drive us all home, or a place that has been waiting for you to name it home; and yes, you will nap lucid in a new un-cynical life of wet pants, bonus drinks, and learning to say yes. Put a towel on the seat. Get in. Take me home. I'm outta words. I'm blanking. Kiss me long war. Kiss me the opposite of cross fit. Kiss me Tennessee porch song. Kiss me assy. Kiss me dead as drugs. Kiss me lost. Kiss me gold in the sunrise. Kiss me all the way home.

TONGUE ON THE WALL
"No one should outlive his power." -John Davidson

Being forgotten is not as bad
as hoping you aren't.
A bridge crosses the Mississippi.
Berryman stands upon it.
The bells spoke.
Feet first.
Beard flipping up
like a tent flap in the breeze.
Jumps.
Misses the water.
Hits the bank.

Hard earth is less scary than dark, forgiving rivers?
Because the soil could push out
what you couldn't?
I write in a library of a dead poet,
a remodeled home in Lenox, Massachusetts,
and I don't know any of the titles on the white shelves.
I feel dumb
as last week when I saw
the first book I ever wrote
in a used bookstore
for a dollar.

I wanted to cry. I tried so hard. All these books
tried so hard.
Now I want to stop, not because someone
abandoned my work, but because
there is just so much
and it really ain't nothin'.
Someone kissed me once and bruised me good and it ain't enough,
and I know what a snowmobile feels like in mid-air and it ain't enough,
and I got lost in sunlight on an island and found unopened wine and
it ain't
enough.

I have a couple of good dream songs that are my best
and it ain't nothin'.
John Berryman's Dad,

shotgun blasting his tongue onto the wood paneling,
how that photo repeated on every page of Berryman's books,
the end of language,
the end of Boy.

John, are you whispering:
you just don't know.
You just don't know
yet.
Poetry didn't take your life.
It kept you here.
It kept you here until you closed your eyes
to the spirits from smokestacks, to the lawns of America,
and grew away from the power of swallowing song-birds
and the hissing fuels of night. You turned away.
Not us.

Did going inside kill you?
I hope you missed the river on purpose.
If you dig at a foundation for too long
the home
will collapse.
John, John, over-read John.
Being forgotten is not as bad
as hoping you aren't.
We hear you every day
and shove you back down.
Stillness,
stillness
ain't nothin'.

GIRL PIZZA AT BACKSPACE IN AUSTIN

No one knows you when you're sober.
No one knows you
when you're too shy to say
hello.

I love seeing beauty,
but I hate learning someone.

Your dress is great.
'I know. I only wear great dresses.'

I smile without letting her see
this new fire.

SOUR MASH

and so you hit the road with some other white poets
and you washed diner dishes in Dallas for a discount on your meal
and they passed the hat around the audience
and you made 50 bucks
and you bought everyone pancakes at Norm's
and years later you hit the road alone
and they paid you 200 bucks
and you bought yourself a dozen loseable sunglasses
and a flask to make it through the open mic
and then you hit the road
with a queer author and a black dude
and they paid you 1500 each.

and you knew you could make a go of this poetry thing
that sucked at your chicken legs and made you follow
and you saw yourself changed
and you thought this kind of art form
could be medicine
and not just embalming fluid.
and you and the power blonde
put on shows in aquariums
and the audience loved it
but they didn't buy much
and you only sold two shirts and three books
and you tried going big and began opening up for rock bands and comics
and you learned that dancing and laughing
had a higher market value than metaphor
and you took the gigs, all the gigs as the gorgeous talked through your sets
and licked the love in their phones
and you took the job reading your work at the party clubs
and read to a room that mingled around the images that broke your ass
and your stack of ideas sold nothing as someone told you
that you were great ambience.

Ugh. You never wanted to be ambience.
and you applied for the grants
and wondered what you'd get to do
if you
won them all,
but you lost them all

and the publisher tried to teach
you that real life sells, unless it's needy
and is often too offensive to sell books
and to go learn the truth
that makes people cheer.

the truth between strangers:
the weather.
listen to how we feel about the weather.
write about the moon
but not about how it fucks up our blood.
and no one wanted to
risk their book sales
by talking about what we all
talked about at the bar.

you all lied to the interviewer when she said:
have you ever had a million horrible thoughts at once?
have you ever wanted to murder someone short?
have you ever realized you were lying about love onstage?
have you ever wanted to die because of how you used to be/are?
have you spent more time writing about living than doing it?

and some of you and your friends got so turned on
by the hunt for evil people, the detestable, the black energy of losers,
you stayed erect for days
and wrote 'everyone is wrong'
with your gleaming cocks and perfect nipple ink.
and some of your friends realized that loneliness was power
and they slipped away.

and some of your friends realized that loneliness was power
and they slipped away.

and some of you and your remaining friends
kept writing inspirational
'hang in there' pieces
cause the rest was too hard to live off of
and the nasty was making us lose fans
and we didn't write anything broken, fuck-heavy, cheap or dirty anymore
and we justified it because we really wanted this one bastard art form
to reach the masses and change the world, or at least a township
because we thought it was better,
we knew a great line of poetry was a bullet and novels were a long choke
and no one had time anyway for real phone calls or involved dinners
so we nailed the fast power of today by turning to poetry
but we poets only argued online amongst ourselves
and pretended that it mattered.
we glowed like we could change the world from an anonymous laptop.

the reviews came in:
your poetry didn't change anything—
it just moved the monster
to the other side of the room.
you thought about real estate sales and finally eating well
you thought about sheep wrangling residencies where your hands
become soil
you thought about being a motorcycle mechanic
that actually fixes something—
anything to feel real and stop wondering
about capturing the 'you don't know what.'
to fuck when you want to and not
ponder the beauty.
to drink when you need to
and not unlock the diary.
to wander in the woods and not
look through the pines
for a great closing line.

to have an internal fuck you every time
you look at trees and say
yes, they are beautiful...but they are not mobile.
what does that mean about me?

morning dew ain't day tears,
storms are not angel farts,
cum is not the dying, drying frost of love.
you used to think poetry was important only to poets,
and now you know that isn't true.
poetry is important to few poets
is true,
as you loom in the libraries of your fellow writers
and notice that if they own more than 10 poetry books
almost everyone is dead.
writers have a hard time
loving now. So, go.
close it all down.
close it all down
and finish the applications.

then, you get a letter.
someone says they needed
one of the poems you wrote.
not that they liked it. needed it.
you try to laugh it off. You try to say you are making
a little lost thing important. The way the bones of your child
found in a lake can be seen as sticks if you don't know.
you try to see something cynical
in how you feel reading the letter.
but all that comes now is
you feel like taking out the trash
and even though you don't know how to—
you want to skip around like an idiot
the great amnesia sets in. and it's back to—
hello, blue bonnets swaying across wide Texas.
hello, all you animals flying above in the blue, blue laundry.
hello to the quiet someone
who removes darts
from the other side of night
and leaves us with
the many little holes
of surprise light.

MENDER/DESTROYER
for COA

Cristin and I were chatting
about her breakup, her new life,
how everything was brand new
and then—
her chair broke,
and she fell to the floor
like mashed potatoes.
She didn't cry.
She just laid there, stretched out
and looked like an extra waiting
for action to be called in a catastrophe film.

When a poet eats it, they begin sorting out the meaning
of all broken chairs,
of all support
surprising you
and caving in suddenly,
unsure of
what sucks more—the bruise or
having to check chairs for the rest of your life.
I helped her up. Swung open the glass door.
I threw the chair high into the backyard air
and watched it shatter.

"Fuck this chair.
This chair is from the forest of assholes.
This chair can eat my hot fuck and die."
Cristin then quietly went outside barefoot,
collected the pieces from the grass,
and took it into the garage
so she could repair it.

"It didn't break.
I broke it.
I intimately understand how to fix it"

FAVORITE ROLLER DERBY NAMES I MADE UP IN PORTLAND AT CLAUDIAS BAR

for Juliet and The Rose City Rollers

cruela da skill
queen elizabitch the none of your business
rink witherspoon
princess slaya
crash bandikooch
miss guided missle
brasby skills and bash
babe-brahamber tamblyn
mary tyler morgue
hammerpants
boobie howser, m.d.
florence henderscum
urkel, the undertaker
abor-shauna
Lisa

CAKE WEEK

She laid across the grave trying to hug it, trying to will herself into
the ground.
I couldn't believe it still broke her up this hard after so many years.
When someone visits the grave of a loved one, and you don't know
what to do
because you didn't know the deceased,
you look around to see if your name is on any tombstone. You try to
show sympathy.
You hold her and try to tell her that we love the spirit and not the flesh.
Their spirit is always around us.

She will tell you that you are wrong.
Both, Derrick. Both. It's like a painting. We don't love Matisse's paints.
We do love what we saw, what we held, and we can also be amused
by how it got there.
The spirit is just paint. I don't get much from photographs. You
would always
rather go to the museum to see a painting rather than in a book. It might
make me feel good to say I loved their spirit, but I love both. I loved his
woodshop hands. I loved his chipped tooth and skin that looked
pulled down by
the weights in the air. I can miss what I can't see anymore.

What a fucking joke that we have to go away.
It's like giving someone coconut cake
and it becomes their favorite thing
and then someone says you can only have it
for a week
and then never again.
Yeah, but how good
is that week
of cake?

TOODLE LOO

"We don't die, Derrick.
We take breaks from each other.
When we die,
it is a sudden break,
it is a see you later. A toodle loo."
My grandfather would say this
when I asked him if he was going to die.
He hated goodbyes and insisted on all of us saying
toodle loo when leaving
because he didn't think any sad goodbye was any good.
It always felt like a tiny death to him.
Goodbye should make you feel good.
The words toodle loo tried to turn a hard moment
into something goofy.

"You gotta laugh kid. Laughter is lobster.
You can't have lobster every day.
If you did, it becomes hamburger.
You need a break from wonderful
to keep the wonderful, wonderful."
Personally, toodle loo was always way too fancy for me to say
to strangers and clerks at various shops.
"Thanks for shopping at Harley Davidson, Derrick."
Hell yeah, thanks for the new choke and chrome throttle grip.
Toodle loo.

"It's not a big deal to die, Derrick.
You give up your power
if you worry about it too much.
Why give up your power?"
I couldn't go to his funeral.
I felt embarrassed
that I couldn't control
my sadness.
I wish I could have faked it.
When I get a chance to eat lobster,
especially the claw meat,
I close my eyes
and it tastes so good.

MULE BREAKER

come to the blue
and find me.
come to the moss night.
come to the woods
loaded with the OCD
cicadas and their tap shoes.
let's get cumberland river, naked.
red teeth calling.
you broken mule.
I still love you.
who is your armory now?
what songs of ours can you still hear?
the radio tried to sell too much
to keep us listening.
I hear you
in every spinning fan blade.
I sing of the thing I wish
I could see again
if I could fall asleep
in peace
long enough to dream you
the right way.

OUR POISON HORSE

The horse in our field.
The black one.
Our poison horse.
Why would anyone try to poison her?
They think boys wanted the flies on her dead.
That or the boys wanted to see the skin peel.
The pesticide scar,
healing now as the jagged underline
slowly closes daily
on the mare's body,
The underlining of everything awful
about us.

I ask you if there is anything worth saving?
You land me
a kiss so hot
the ferns die.
A grip so tight,
the blisters
keep you from volunteering to carry
anymore coffins.
Broken fast
like an under chucked
snowball.
Lungs rising
like Dresden
steeples.
A kiss so hot
the butcher's meat
is ready.

You are
this coward's
drink,
a last drink
before
the bell rings
and the crowd wants blood
and the rafters spin.
Your face is leaking.

You're the one permanent wedding.
I'm a teenage dog in the back of a truck.
I gotta jump. When will it slow down enough?
You tell me you love me,
and it unfolds my will
to live.

STRANGE LIGHT

LOVERS FIZZ

Remind me of Spain.
Let the propane
light from the barbecue
glow the back of your hair into
silhouette.
Set.
Put bicycle grease on your bedsprings.
Let no one hear your love.
Subtle your lust. Lash it to your spine and walk funny.
Stand in front of the mirror with a camera
waiting for the love of your life to show up.
Drive to me.
Scuttle your plans.
Drive with the radio off.
Drive like a Trucker that's been face-punched.
Peel your car out and shoot gravel back into the sky.
Don't be Amsterdam, be Holland.
I've never been to Spain. I'm asking you to remind me of it.
Don't just be tits, be all the tits, be wanted.
Don't puss out on love.
Put some ice cream in the dead man's float.
You're either someone's dinner or you're someone's genius,
either way doesn't matter as long as you're zizzing delicious.
Allow me to be an ocean, allow me to freeze.
I'm saying I can hold you up,
even the waves retreat to make room for new ones.
I need you to forget all endings that demand paradise.
Your terror moves me. Your failures have whittled you fine.
Scream into the road map until your lungs are transmission hot:
Dear Lord, is that all you got?

Some giant in the sky pushes
the head of night down
into the sea
and a crown of stars bubbles
on up. Fizzle that way.

RINGLETS

Young prom ladies in loud dresses and ringlets
mingle outside the restaurant in oversized
men's suit jackets, their dates, smile-smoking,
shivering, pretending not to shiver. The thing
you said was dead is not dead. No virgin deserves
a cigarette. We should head to the emergency room
and just pop our heads in and say hello. Tell them we
are alright so they don't think we only visit when
things are bad. We are breathing without tubes today.
They don't make pills yet for this feeling. It's like finding fruit
in the snow. I want to call down cocktails and black tire
jacks from the heavens. I want to break into something.
That kind of good. Your eyes are the kind we have all been waiting for.
When I hear a single note sustain in a room
with bad lighting, I think of us.
Both of our bodies,
shivering.

OUR LONG LOW NIGHTS

1.
Sometimes when a jazz cymbal
is played with a brush—
a steady soft roll—
I hear those rainy streets,
the cars I shoved you against,
kissing you into place.
I can hear them coming for us,
rolling across the wet asphalt.
Our shirts as skin, soaked tight.
We both hate poems that mention jazz,
which is okay, because jazz hates us.
We kiss like jazz hates us.
2.
You're not scared of living,
you're not scared of love,
you're not scared of money, sex or the truth,
but there's never enough.
3.
You said life is as short and confusing as a small, angry dog.
It can tell when you're afraid of it. If you open your hand towards it
and it snaps for blood
it is correct to punch it hard in the neck.
4.
Walk to the grocery store and play "Find the worst shampoo smell."
"Find the least sexiest peanut butter."
"Find the in store announcement microphone
and see who can quote hip-hop lyrics the longest
using manager voice."
Buy a month's worth of paper plates.
Try to not let grief be as easy as pajamas all day.
5.
In the cupboard I find corn silk powder.
When I am bored, I sprinkle some out on the floor and Bing Crosby
in my socks.
It makes me miss the skin on the insides of your legs.
6.
You found a sledgehammer in the garage.
Someone with a sledgehammer loves me.
I rejoiced like Berlin.

We invented a game called Find Two Things to Smash.
We played it every night. Whoever found the most "I should've smashed that a long time ago" thing,
doesn't have to clean up. You want me to write you a book of these sounds.
Here.
7.
The kind of love that matters is
walking into the China shop with a 2x4 and waiting for the nervous clerk to say, "…can I help you?"
Then saying, "No, but I can help you."
8.
When your chest is heavy and full of colorful medals from the day,
I'll have beers and bath waiting.
If we don't have a bath, I'll find our biggest bowl.
9.
A horsewhip snaps—the sound barrier is broken. Even the laws of nature, even us.
10.
The poetry class taught me to start strong, end strong.
I am supposed to write down the greatest thing about you,
that I could imagine about you.
We ordered pizza.
We told our friends we couldn't meet up.
There were cherries and bourbon sauce in the fridge.
You dragged our mattress into the living room.
Turned out all the lights.
Watched an actor try too hard.
The phone didn't ring.
The commercials were funny.
I ran my fingernails down your arm.
We forgot napkins.
Studied the way windows make you look at them
instead of out them
when rain gives in.
Nothing was on.
Nothing is on.

THE BEST or MANIAC SOUL PLUMBER

Texas is Jacuzzi fat.

Texas is lost in you,
in the mosquito dark.

Thank you dead Texas,
for putting the claim on my love.

Secede from Texas.
Come back to me, dear.

Come back to deer meat.
Texas is too hot and wide to be hugged.

I can't afford to touch you when you are in Texas.
Is your Christmas card going to be the entire death penalty?

Are you going to wear jeans that make your vagina plural?
Are you going to take pride in suicide being an outdoor nap?

Are you going to learn to not apologize for Abilene,
for it being as empty and weird as us?

Come back to me.
We can move to the pale Northwest.

Portland can't stop cloud crying.
Bend Oregon is pretty nice if you like Californians.

Here
is best.

WHEN NURSES COUGH

When I first heard the nurse cough
I thought man,
she must not be very good at her job.

STRAY LIGHTNING

The feeling inside,
when you know there's fireworks,
but you're head's so heavy
you can't look up.
I know this hair is a dead willow mess,
this hair is Ally Sheedy in a staged blizzard and
these pants pretend that celibacy is boring.
I'm often shirtless. I embarrass nature.
I know a vegetarian who eats horseradish
and doesn't think that's funny.
I don't get offended easy, I don't get easy enough.
I know the hard life of being a writer can leave you severely
dramatized.
Stare down the sky long enough and learn why lightning is as jagged
as us.
Try and imagine how many will adore you and find out that math
is death.
I blow my money on magic no one else may see.
I stand at the back of punk shows, and church fog machine spectacles,
and poetry readings,
waiting for someone to make me bouquet.
I know now I wasted much of my young life
putting up a wooden fence
around the volcano.
I know why people compare their lovers to ballrooms.
I need a suit.
I'll write my own invitation.

INSTEAD OF KILLING YOURSELF

wait until
a year from now
where you say,
"Holy fuck,
I can't believe I was going to kill myself before I etcetera'd...
before I went skinny dipping in Tennessee,
made my own IPA,
tried out for a game show,
rode a camel drunk,
skydived alone,
learned to waltz with clumsy old people,
photographed electric jellyfish,
built a sailboat from trash,
taught someone how to read,
etc. etc. etc."
The red washing
down the bathtub
can't change the color of the sea
at all.

NO WALLS, NO GO

After the soft coals of sleep
the scratching at my bedroom door returns,
-the old, familiar Wolf-Fox of Sorrow,
blood in paws, low crawl in the grass,
he has come again.
To crawl back inside me and weave himself in.
To chew out my insides and sew himself in.
The terrible sewing.

I woke up yesterday morning and
wanted to blow my brains out,
with a shotgun.
Two shells to blow my brains on the most beautiful wall—
the cleanest wall — a pool of milk waiting at the base—
the starkest white: eggshell or matte.
Spinning while exploding.
The mad spin. Walls catching me. Pink pink pink.
I am fine with being the last of my name.

When I awake in our bed, hungry for these exit songs,
there is dust splitting the light.
There is that gaudy sky, all roofs on the ground,
and there are no walls for miles.
There is only rubble, settling dust, and a breeze.
You are standing there above me
with sledgehammer...exhausted.
Exhausted. Your shirt, a creek of sweat.
Your chest shining like a Colt Peacemaker.
Your voice is cashmere and rescue.
You say,
"My dear, true love is labor.
I will not learn how to love the dead.
No walls, no go.
There is nowhere to hang a calendar.
There is nowhere for clocks.
My love is for the living."

This page is a little break for you to drink water.

JOY IN PLACES WITHOUT YOU

Northfield, Minnesota is pastel quiet,
is without your strut,
your lovely saffron gust and mint smoke.
I am glad you are not here. Northfield is smell.
On the east side, in the Malto-meal plant
they're making thousands of boxes
of knock-off breakfast cereals that sound like bad love tricks:
Tootie Fruities, Coco-roos, Honey Nut Scooters, Corn Bursts,
Blueberry Muffin Tops, Nut Buzzers, Golden Puffs,
and coming soon, Cheerful Circles.
I'd love to walk into the office,
barefoot and hollering
that I bit into a cheerful circle.
On the west side,
they're slicing the softest turkey necks,
cutting off the feathery haunches,
melting down the gluey bones.
The sorrowful smell collision goes right into my Lager.
I am drinking the greatest slaughter this season. The smell is
becoming me.
I am here at the rube-n-stein pub
making this for you.
This cheap photography,
warp and scribble.
Slow and warm in the birch walls
under the dumb paintings,
the TV sound, the famous TV light,
showing people falling off of chairs and an audience dressed
like Mormons,
laughing like someone told them to.
The smell I miss is you, the thing I become.
Yes, I know it is the worst thing to say to a lover:

I miss all your smells.
I ponder what they really are
cause they aren't impossible saffron, or new lemons, or cinnamon
sex mix.
It could just be soap. I miss your soap.
I can't name it. Why do tears come?
I believe I am happy

and don't
know what to do with it.
I'll let it all slide down my face
and drop onto my tongue.
I sing the words:
How will I ever go back from here?

STRANGE LIGHT

0- Darkness.
0- Voice.
Here is the story of one man with strange light
and tiny blisses.
a story of wild me
lost among wild you.
I wanted to be down in the obscene with you.
I wanted to see it all.
To leave the black, slow sea of the heavens.
How empty and pure peace can be.
Days with no end.
Navigating celestially.
Bored to life.
I wanted to be with you.
To taste warm blue
waves of deep salt.
The council of the heavens asked me why I wanted to descend
into the territory of those
gloriously unplugged buzzards.
I told them I wanted the song of amazement horrible.
The plush rest of joy.
The sensations of a spirit mended and becoming aware. Those
living things.
To holler among the living.
To holler under the afternoon rainstorm juice.
To cheer on that ballerina tornado
who finally gets to let it all out.
To watch the house lift away
and feel better, tornado.
To feel the kiss of a drunk dog and say, "I know. I know."

To hunt God. To wash the mud from my gun
after finding him hiding in the soil.
To put his bloodied head on my wall.
To hunger in my veins for a No trophy life. No trophy love.
To succeed at floating when people urge me to sink.
To fail at hotel bed diving.
To fall for the night buzz and sudden bugs of writing,
that cheap photography.
To smell smoke nearby when I am cold.

To grieve the way I couldn't imagine grieving.
To grieve alone and feel my muscles
growing from it.
To have one choice and choose poorly.
To be thrown from the car crash and wait in the tree-line,
listening to crickets strumming for help.
To undo the face of my enemy.
To love them silently.
To aim my lung cannons for fascination and burst into violin.
The mouth awaiting someone versed in sparkler,
the heart singing a sustain of piano blood.
I want sunlight to learn me. To learn my shape.
To learn why a bomb sings one note as it falls through the air.
My shape breaking the air.
Colors bursting forth of blood-oranges, fog and honey? Yes, those colors.
I am coming down there.
I am ready to wrap my future arms around it all.
I want to dance wolf-skinny under the bald moon.
The eggshell moon.
The quarter moon that looks like an Arabic shoe.
That moon. That beat up moon,
lifting higher like a balloon from a child's buttery hands.
The looming, foaming moon,
tired of being written down or dreamily discussed.
I will find out why it returns and who it returns for.

Let it gleam across me. Doing its job. I can see it all.
I want to hold the face of my lover
and then watch their hair turn beautiful as they drift away.
To marvel at young unwanted boners,
that stupid bullhorn in the trousers. Yeah, yeah.
To applaud the loosened old man skin,
allowing room for weakness.
To welcome light as the next shift.
To watch it slip away
and not know much.
To wonder about it all and know that it was good.
To know that it was good and that it was all.
To marvel at the journey of impossible lovers.
To notice the trophy missing from my wall
and know that God can be found and can escape.
For all this is worthy of experience.

The experience of undoing and becoming.
My plea was for a taste. My plea was granted.
I fell to earth
and saw what Lucifer saw on his way down.
It was beautiful enough to break even the blackest of hearts.
0- Speed.
0- Descension.
1- I was born as a small surprise of light.
Low budget Christmas tree light.
I had a heart full of volume and grizzly bear drool.
A loud little spaz. Born hollering.
I was screaming that I made it! I made it! Can't believe I made it.
I'm here on earth you huge fuckers!

Deliver me. Clean me up. Nothing could shut my brass mouth up.
My cries meant: Team, You can swing your limbs in the air
like a spermy idiot and cry out that your boy is born!
Swim on swimmers!
My Mother relieved to have the blob out of her.
Proud as a peach pie.
When I was born, my father swung around like a broke machine,
our harmony of uncontrollable screaming: he yelled:
my boy is born, my boy is born,
my boy is born, my boy is born-
and no one gets to touch it... him.
My Father said, "I have a suitcase full of all the things I could not be.
I can not wait to dress him in all of it."
My light was more of my Mother's and it was once shining and correct.
It was.
It was.
3- Riding upon Father's shoulders, teeth closer to the sun.
5 -Mother tells me that someone bright will love me,
just not as much as her.
6 - Father says, Son, look at the field.
People will come to build on you or burn you out. Look at the sea.
Anchors can hold a ship, or hold it back.
Our kitchen cupboard full of lost jobs. A house of separate beds.
When I was young, my Father dressed me in all the wrong clothes.
The holes in my jeans were advent calendars.
I was afraid a lot.
Afraid of the devil chasing me in my dreams,
afraid of devils in helicopters...devils with lasers.

I was also afraid of the dark.
My father was red lights and tall blue grass.
I was afraid, afraid of the punishment
of the swinging belt in the dark.
I was afraid of pulling down my pants and getting the belt
the wooden spoon, the plum branch, the belt buckle
in the dark.
Not knowing when the swing was coming,
or where it would make contact,
my Father would say, "Don't you ever do that again."
Swinging with each "ever."
Fury coloring his skin in rubies.
I wonder when rage first bit his ankles and filled his Texas blood.
I wonder why it doesn't find me. I wonder if it is waiting.
I know that when I am older, I might not want kids—
maybe so there is no one for me to unload or rev upon.
I'll marry the dark.
When the dark comes I will party in it.
I will make it silly. I will keep my light.
I wrote to my Father last year
that I wanted to know his life—
asked him if he was dating, and how his back was.
He wrote
"May God richly bless you…"
It ended with ellipses. As if he was going to add something
like, "…for me, he did not…"
"May God richly bless you…"
Grief had stolen many of his words.
I see him as a man who tried
and is tired of the trying.
A man with bags and bags of ellipses'.
I could not fit into his clothes.
His days are waiting for things to grow dim,
wondering if this is what he was made for,
the end, pulling him like a gondola cable.

I sleep in the day.
The belts I see in stores are something to me now,
small noose,
devil's tails,
horse whipped to death.
I try to fill my head with Christmas.

I asked for a telescope for Christmas
when I was young
so I could see far from where I was.
A place to wait for rain
or any kind of storm.
A tornado that removes everything.
I hear his voice sometimes say,
"...except for you and your sister, eh... I dunno...I dunno...
may God richly bless you."
10 - Rode my bike face first into the washing machine
and felt my bones come alive.
11 - Started to say the word "Shit" comfortably.
14 - Got the "Shit" kicked out of me for what I called was creative
dissidence.
One day, when I felt as alone as the Hawaiian Islands
I decided I didn't want to be afraid anymore.
I was getting older, lankier and felt different
like one tasty pear in a pile of pomegranates.
At school they tried to tell me:
DON'T DO ANYTHING DIFFERENT!
DON'T DO ANYTHING DANGEROUS OR FRILLY!
DON'T SEARCH TOO FAR OR YOU WILL BE BURIED!
DON'T REVEAL THAT WHICH IS SCARY!
And a few teachers cried:

But
the kids got heart
I think this kids got heart
no no no no no
What if this kids got heart
Let him out
no no no no
Stand up
Up straight
Straight back
Hold still
Fashion lips tight
Soften the voice,
Unhard your stare
Mind manners
Tuck your derriere
Fair skin

No muscle
Gas face
No seconds
Little boy
Little boy
Stop crying for water
Little boy little boy
Stop crying for water
Submissive turkey legs, you with the chicken arms,
your face looks like animal hell.
What a fashion collapse!
Someone un-perm his curly brain.
Sit up
Here's the continuation of the poems:

Suck down
Back straight black nape
Clean your neck
Wash your ass
Chin up, chow down
Hold still cradle, cradle, cradle
Sit up straight
Stand like a man, we have made plans, huh what?
Never tell a lie-
you just keep inventing answers
Stop crying for water
Stop dreaming of dancers
lifting you away, good luck motherfucker
But the kids got heart
no no no no
This kid thinks Jesus' blood was diet coke!
Don't' talk in rewind, boy
Don't eat the phone
Don't bite table, boy!
Your rough will be honed
Do not vomit light!

Don't kiss the engine when it is running
Don't draw visions of death on your final exam, whoa boy!
Do not stare death at its entrance, smiling what, shut up!
Don't get gashey
Don't try and out-spin our throwing knives

Don't show off, don't show on, don't Chopin! Don't Gershwin!
Don't this kid got heart?
No No No!
You listen to me turkey legs, here's the deal.
There seems to be something unnatural revving inside you.
It could be an elephant on a bicycle. We are not sure.
There is something big inside
this little puke.
It may be losing its balance,
something elaborate inside him, something elaborate inside this
little puke.
It will never do.
But don't the kid got heart? The crowd screams.
The boy says, I think so.
It is best we let him go.

Boy says,
"...let go or be dragged, light suckers."
Everyone stares in his eyes and boy says, "Wow, you can't show me
shit city,
I'm the motherfucking mayor. Flush."
Maybe we send him back into the imploding zoo of the metropolis,
where he can get more lost,
commanding the street lights.
Let him scream spazzfucky unto those golden beams,
befriending the archers in the shadows, cleaning his ears
with the harmless ends of arrows,
hearing all the rules wrong,
doomed with the wasted and poor,
hearing the hum of desire,
the air filters of cooling imagination-
jotting it all down for what?
No manners. No success. No timing. What if he becomes nothing?
He does have heart
and that is only worth a glass of water. Give him a drink. Let him go.
What a puke, fantastic.
16 - I tried to not break under the rickety tables of religion,
the walls of rules. My light, damp and bare.
18 - Kissed a girl in a theater play. Wanted to be in every play.
22 - Alone and proud of alone. Mad at lovers who locked their
fingers together, sunset eyes, citrus women AND discount
FLOWER SHOPS.

Later, in my twenties, I was army,
then I was lonely as museum treasure,
then I felt free.
In the great outside, she found me.
She was wearing too many colors to be taken seriously.
was in my 20's and posing like Hemingway's valet.
Calling Paris and telling it was over.

Drinking and wishing I knew how to fight with my pants down.
Wondering how to claw my way into a dress
since "talent" wasn't working.
Proud of my dim light. My very dim and dimming light.
She arrived like lost mail.
She didn't trust anyone barefoot.
She wasn't afraid of anything.
Lonely too, but not tragic. She was Margaret.
Margaret's heart had no crust.
Smelled like wet black cherries.
A woman born with a capacity for sunbursting.
That was my Margaret.
Hair of dirty tinsel, brown and furious.
Her hands were branding irons and I soon became hers.
Off to the park with a flask full of anesthesia.
The snails rolled up inside their shells,
rocking back and forth against each other.
This was a glossy summer, everything was in love.
Our hearts spread eagle and searched, thoroughly.
I had never heard the word splendor
come out of a girls mouth before.
I heard it when she was asleep.
She told me she still saw something
flickering in me and that it was enough to keep her warm.
It was enough.
We were not star-crossed, we were horny music.
The scorn of the boring.
Dressed as a classic red rose, she lived in the teeth of the matador.
The other roses dying in expensive vases.
What kind of woman draws a survival manual for the wilderness
in case it was attacked by humans?

Spiders weren't scared around her, and didn't feel scary around her.
She longs for the ocean to freeze solid so we can slide to Ghana and

vanish, into cocoa and gold coast.
A falcon dives at 200 mph.
A human can run up to 27 miles per hour.
I am slow love.
I move at the speed of bad mood lighting.

She still moved towards my poverty and loved me for years.
I loved her with all my heart.
I loved her with all of everyone's heart.
I said, "I may not love you forever Margaret.
But I will try with all of my weird might for as long as the day will allow."
Everything is supposed to die.
It does not frighten me now.
26 - Lived in the mountains. I grew a beard.
It did not make me smart or savage, just dirty and delicate for frost.
27 - Searchlights and hot cardamom formed in my passion.
I loved Margaret in a crazy fashion.
As time passed, our love progressed into other levels.
I'd see Margaret's body and I would not know what to do with it.
Then all of a sudden… I did know what to do with it. And it was nice.
Our breath, shoving.
Our lips, doin' the blossom.
A woman in a bra is like seeing a hammer
nailed to a wall. My pants full of nails.
She crosses her legs and keeps crossing them
until she is wound up like a Bavarian pretzel.
I blow on her windward side.

She spins into the ground like a drill
She asks me, as I describe it, if I wrote wound or wound.
She wants to know what the readers will think.
I see her pink dregs,
her fast healing,
her righteous sweets,
her knees and ankles in knots.
She is nervous, marvelous, deep in the dirt.
Winding up and unwinding like a sweater that cannot make up its mind.
I felt loose as hell's door and it was good.
She was porn for dead girls.
She was a refrigerator full of synthetic blood
in a reckless town. I think of birds when she is near.
I imagine the worms last sensations

as it lifts up into the air,
feeling its first breeze, flying in the ravens mouth.
O how she carries me, as the soon devoured.
Will you fade Margaret? Like a magazine left in the window?
I can not unlace you from my head.
Margaret gave her days to me and we bloomed into bright years.
How we bloomed.

"Soon we will all be dust and poorly lit photography."

Particles of dust, they too catch light.
39 - Joy. Spent all our money on dumb stuff and launched it off the roof, laughing like crows.
41 - We never married. We should have. I should have. I could never say why.
44 - I blew out my back at work. I tried painting. I was terrible. I became terrible.
48 - We parted. I miss her. I beat the feeling into the walls. I'm glad she left, for her sake.
49 - God has richly blessed me…
49
57
68
72
As an older man,
I had a dream about walking backwards through devastation,
a destroyed place,
realizing at the end of the poem that I did it.
The good news was that I could see things growing
once the soil had been tilled by my explosions.
There were signs littered about, some said No loitering.
Some said—
No proof
No baster
No finger twitch
No soft metal ballad
No yellowing in the eyes
No sissy strut
No love letter drag
No shoes repaired

No finger twitch
No soft metal ballad
No yellowing in the eyes
No sissy strut
No love letter drag
No shoes repaired

No burning fire escape
No wedding march with sirens
No fever kiss
No rosy easy funeral
No brawl for her
No reason to hold your fingernails in your teeth
No staying power for things in flight
No binocular peep show
No day nakedness
No lust laid upon you like your favorite jacket
No cloud cover Sunday bliss
No shade in the desert
No anchors for battered vessels
No black smokers below
No signs of the end
No signs on the road
No end, No road
No markings on the road
No now
I'm 49
The night is coming, the great night, falling slow and easy.

The night is coming, the great night, falling slow and easy.
I'm 57
The wind moves toward me like a coffin on a luggage carousal.
I'm 68
The dark is possible, the dark is always possible.
People falling in it everyday.
Margaret's passing hit me like poison,
like I had been drinking it all my life and finally let it work.
I'm 72
I am tired and fading.
49
57
68

The night is coming, the great night, falling slow and easy.
I'm 57
The wind moves toward me like a coffin on a luggage carousal.
I'm 68
The dark is possible, the dark is always possible.
People falling in it everyday.
Margaret's passing hit me like poison,
like I had been drinking it all my life and finally let it work.
I'm 72, I am tired and fading.

73 - I will not die. I can not die. I will myself this life. I must keep writing myself down.
No pine tar heart!
No costume armor parade!
No graceful widows walk!
No sissy strut emergency room,
No hard star glimmer in my eye.
No white light dream sequence.
Fuck you. Death. Fuck you.
No sequin sorrow shining from within me.
Hurrah Hurrah these ghosty places.
Hurrah Hurrah these places I have walked upon and who have walked upon me.
Hurrah Hurrah the drunk calligraphy of two bodies
still unfurling in my mind.
Margaret, Margaret. My luminous Margaret.
Margaret, your nervous laughter feels like home.
I sing of your sudden lust, your smashed glamour, broken chest custodian, memory thief,
your ease in fumbling for the things I needed,
things I could never retrieve.
Every mansion in this town is bored, Margaret.
Every mansion in heaven.
All their closets full of shiny skeletons.
They will never play our music. Never.
The angel of death at the wrong cocktail party? Early to help set up?
Fuck you.
I must keep you alive in my head Margaret.
I loved your full resume.
I loved your throaty kiss.
I am gushing.
I am ready to fill this night with senseless acts of
ha cha cha, no retreat, no quarter.
I'm going berzerker.
I ain't goin' west

like death.

I am still tornado ballet. Still longing to lift you away.
Hurrah Hurrah your shadow that finds rest inside me.
Hurrah Hurrah the fight, the unwinnable fight that seems winnable.
Hurrah Hurrah us loyal dogs.
Hurrah Hurrah the echo that is not forever.
Hurrah Hurrah the things that do not last.
Hurrah Hurrah the night, the naked, and the poor
floating upon it.
I will not let my story be held hostage.
I want it to be haunted.
I want chance to flow in through the windows
like a Baptist miracle flood.
I could not will this poem into life.
This is what it wanted to say to you.
I am sorry in six dead languages.
The no poetry of I am sorry,
the lost volumes of I am sorry.
This is more. This is all of it, Margaret.
I am sorry for wanting what I was
and I know you are sorry for wanting that too.
I tried to blow my chest out
with a flashlight,
the hearts chunky mess waiting for illumination.
Your arms turned me bulletproof.
Is this you?
Your light, my beacon, the river shining a way out.
The tar pits of night are sucking me in.
All hail the ships
that sail beyond dusk
without wind.

All love is love in the dark.
All love is love in the dark.
I fought. I am coming home.
When we die
it is poetry
that leaves the body…

DERRICK BROWN'S FAMOUS LAST WORDS

Most snakes are friendly if you don't surprise them.
Is that all the wasabi you got back there?
Would it be possible to join the gang
just for the summer?

UH-OH

EVERY COFFIN IS A SOAP BOX DERBY

Tear apart every picture frame in the house and build that casket.
Wallpaper the roof of it with the photos
like your high school locker.
Load it with the images of all the animals and friends you loved.
Lie down in it with a new bullhorn,
letting them know that you blew it,
that what you 'knew' was wrong and it's fine,
that you should have planned less, undressed and just begun.
You should have been more strolling grateful
and less city of butt-rock and boring piss.

Holler gratefulness to the animals you killed
or that died around you, under your care, trying to make you see.
Thank you for the master class.

Should've watched and learned
that language doesn't solve everything,
to fight at the right time, to surrender well,
to hold still and shake alone, clean your nasty out and eat it wild,
race down the grass on ice blocks
and howl away nude in the night
realizing that untamed is the better solution.

Look at you. You're racing away. The lid still open.
The details whiz by and you reach out to catch them,
but it's all flash paper.

You will gain speed and sing that the prize is wildness.
Chop up all them frames,
let yourself be scared as a pheasant realizing the decoy,
too late, too late.

Pack the bags under your gaze.
Get into your solid black soap box derby for one.
Goodbye clean heroes. Goodbye marketable life.
Goodbye… safe lethargy. Goodbye resurrected shame.
Goodbye wallflower botanist.
Roll away proud. Sing out that you are not sorry.

Forever is for losers.

You have got to go.
Why not leave in a Champion face?
Cross the finish line and freeze in that Champion face.
Goodbye. You win. Close the lid.
It's getting warm.
Look how the racer becomes a finish line.
Relax and give in to all the victoriously beautiful,
loving energies of death.

ETHERNET BALLAD
For Eugene and Katie

I first plugged her in.
Her report clearly states:
My Man.
My generous heart.
Champion of the odd.
Tear loofah.

I'm sorry the world doesn't want a TV show
called Horseback Surprise.
I do.
You solve my loneliness and lo-fi fear.
I'll make you a cocktail when you are down
with a jigger of cold beach
and a splash of helium
to lift your chin
when the forces of hmphf
are against you.

Shall I hide in the house before you get home
to scare the heavy day off of you?
I will. Your boo is meant to be scary.
Look at me and hear the jukebox of us.
Look at me and hear 1956 shooting out of my poodle.
See me eating shit, flail dancing at every sock hop.
See me parallel parking every Chevy Bel Air like a boss.

My Man.
My reservoir of kindness.

I'd steal plot specific things
from every movie set to make you laugh.
I demand a rewrite.
I demand your kiss, French theft.
You have stolen me in broad daylight.
You have a search light face
and it still shines hot
from my tiny palaces.

Then I plugged in the man.

His readout suggests:
CSSSSHHHHHHH.
Ribs. Bye bye.
CSSSSSHHHHHHH.
Scotch. Ow. Mmm.
CSSSSHHHHHHH.
Lady lady lady lady lady lady lady
cool buns lady lady lady
Lady lady.

My tandem swimmer.
My body pillow with veins.
Where I retreat and fall back in the war of myself.
Did you know all snakes dream of karate?
They wake up sobbing
and can't wipe the tears away?
Everyone wants a love
like a roundhouse to the neck
but not everyone is lucky in legs.

I dunno.
I'm crazy as a cranberry.
CSSSHHH.
I need to send a complaint letter to
Sharper Image for quitting too early.
Lady, I won't quit.
I'll marry your feet.
I'll eat 50 dollars.
You know I can do it.

I am psyched by your love.
I am also psyched by horseradish.
Shall I hold you like a ship's wheel
as the winds rise around us?
We should get some plants.

STROKER OF SORROW

Pushing this boat through the slow easy,
black gondola steady
like a coffin
on a luggage carousel. A line I've written before.
Everyone is in love on my ship
in love with the dark
because the dark is possibility.

No hard star glimmer above.
No sequin sorrow on the dresses of the horny.
Just slow stroker of sorrow
through the syrup of the canals.
Should I sing? I should sing. Tip or no tip.
Hoorah hoorah these ghosty places.

Hoorah hoorah the drunk calligraphy of two bodies
unfurling before me in a Mexican blanket.
Hoorah hoorah nervous laughter that feels like home.
Hoorah hoorah sudden lust and fumbling
for things on the floorboard
that won't be retrieved.

Slipping past the echoes of the Ravenna bridge.
All these mansions are bored. Money skeletons and mink blur coats.
The heads of animals, the ones they wished they could've killed on their own,
mounted for that unique kind of pride
that makes the knowing chuckle.
They will never play our music
in these mansions.

Stare at these sizzling and magic lovers before you,
their hearts full enough for the capsize of love,
down to fall for each other's full resume.
All hail these swollen weirdos,
these bruised lip mongrels and misplaced lovers.
The ones born at the wrong time with the bowlegs and odd shapes.

The "give this to me now or I'll eat your dumb cheeks" summoners.
The throaty kiss slingers who have waited so long for a

semi-private gush.
Fill this night with senseless acts of ha-cha cha. Go wild.
Say the first thing that you want as loud as you can.
So the last thing you want very quietly.

Hoorah hoorah that I just plain felt good tonight
among the tight arms of lovers.
Hoorah hoorah
that it is true as light coming from the water and solid
as this steady warming mansion lamps.
Heaven can keep 'em.
Someone is singing in confused gibberish.
Thank God he keeps singing our song.

Hoorah hoorah staying power you loyal dogs.
Hoorah hoorah the bridges puckering for our entrance.
Hoorah hurrah these echoes that are not forever.
Hoorah hoorah the night, the naked and poor
floating upon it.

BLIZZARD

All the people who still sing after swallowing broken bottles.
All the camp counselors who earned their insomnia for the things
they hide.
All the bug-eyed audiences of loving freaks.
All the haunted creeps of America holding you in the arms of their
weed couches.

All the heart in the frat boy who shared his sandwich after I got jumped.
All the lovers who hated me because I sucked out the little they had left.
All the lovers who waited for us to meet again.
All the ice locked in the woman who kissed you with her hair loaded
in smashed pearls of snow.

You're going to get it all and you may leave here empty.
I am not going to tell you everything.
I wanted gusto, just like you. I wanted blood, love and travel,
but I was too afraid to quit my job. I am still afraid, but I did it and
I don't know if it's a better life.

I got jobs off and on, but the spark
to write was true because when the money vanished I had to keep
doing it.
I chased and hunkered down in the rambling feelings of my
favorite books of poetry,
to travel when I had enough bread and let myself be open to the anguish
of falling for someone who lived far away.

I wanted someone bright to come at me, and to come at me with
spirit—to do the work on me.
I knew they were waiting out there, somewhere.
I wanted to feel the church of booze and debate,
the church of no-guilt, the church of inclusion and anti-tragedy,
the hymns forever sung in the church of sexual madness..

Hello. It Doesn't Matter

FIRST SKINNY DIP

Are you sure, Jo?
Before she answered, her sleek, naked body vanished into the
night waters of Key West.
Her body— a summer luxe, unfair, dragging ivory piano moonlight
into the sea with her.
Careful, Jo. I see lightning bursting about a mile to the horizon.
She laughed and swam farther out, away from the back deck of the
old Chris-Craft watching me become smaller.

I had missed the sway and rock of my former little ship, The Sea Section.
The best August sway and noon naps of my life. The worst damp winters
    of my life.
Hours earlier we roared the Super Chief through the hot Florida rain
until the island Keys ended and we arrived at our dumpy but sturdy little
    ship rental
to sleep on for the night.

This is a bad idea. Storm's closing in. Electricity and water, it's so
dumb to…
Jo's blond hair salt-slicked back just her eyes exhorting.
I took off my shirt, standing in swim trunks, embarrassed of my
tour body,
my hands octopussing around the ashamed drink tickets of my gut.

What's the jellyfish situation? Aren't you freezing? Do you want
your bottoms? I've never done this before.
Jo laughed. "You've never skinny dipped? You gotta just jump in. Live
a little. There's no one out here."
I hate being naked.
"C'mon. You look fine."

I was glad she didn't say amazing. My trunks slinked to the deck.
I counted to three and jumped stiff, legs out, paratrooper style.
The water, a sloshing chalkboard. The night, cracking.
She came to me, lifevesting around my shoulders. "See? Not so bad."

It feels kind of good. I am worried a fish is gonna swim up my ass,
a little dirty fish.
I'm worried we're gonna get fried by lightning. Tell me Jo, how do
you not care?

"I used to be a scared person. Then bad stuff. Maybe 'cause I've been through so much bad.
I think you are either free after tons of bad or you are living pre-bad and have no idea of the bad that awaits you.
I'm French pressing the shit out of every good drop of the rest of this life."
The night air was nothing. She hung on me and I didn't sink.
The lightning, flashbulbing in the distance.

YOU WERE ONCE THE SIZE OF A THUMB

I tried to convince everyone my heart was a golden rosary, but I found out it was just anal beads.
Gimme a chaos.
I am vessel lost. Eater of dead starlight. Clear as a cult.
I paid attention to the breeze and I am broke for it.
I am energized by darkness, like a reporter's voice.
I forget everyone I meet was once thumb-sized and pure.

Gimme pure chaos.
I need a champion who can curse like a savior. I need a job.
I'll need a new job when I get that job. I am a job, and you can do this job on drugs.

I was once thumb-sized. Then, the size of a potato sack wishing for a waterbed.
I thought the waterbed would never get old. It did. I did.
I lived proud and alone on that holy sea.
My raft of small weapons couldn't stop the Angel of Eternity
from running me aground.
I continue my savior hunt. If he bleeds, he leads.

If I am lost at sea, I would like to know. Gimme a signal.
I know you paint a bicycle white and chain it to the spot where the rider died.
Be more careful with each other. Why do I feel at home in a city full of white bicycles?
I sail on in a city of white bicycles.

A woman full of resurrection reaches for me: Are you my rescue?
When she leans in, drunk, kiss sounds like chaos.
Gimme a chaos, Derrick. Gimme a big fat chaos.
Her hailing eyes.
In them I see the violent future
I see us pushing through and you are a feeling
and I belong to it.

NIGHTSTAND MUSIC

Your flight suit unzipped in a heap
Deadly legs smoked in jet fuel
Leather gloves undoing my spine

Where'd you come from?
You point up face all pleased and haunting like a trophy
Tits tightening stiff in my sock
An orchard in napalm

Strengthen my tongue into you
Not drag, but drink rose water fresh bursting across your lazy lips
You may love your family but you are from nowhere when cumming
Master me
Squeezing your feet as your grind out a month of loneliness into me
Fragrant pusher— a meadow of color in your cheeks
a force of tingles rising as my tongue slides up the center of your golden hours
Sweat of eyeliner

All the linen erased

Scream out like a movie theater fire
Open the windows
Let the lost tune in
Legs long as a week in Huntsville
Transmit the power
Trigger willows to explode

Out-sass the purple jacaranda, botanical elegance, immoral and fine
The great salted butter of letting go
A laughter of one absurd body learning an absurder body
Prey upon me
Devour this crumbling that longs to destroy you nightly
Your bra twist-torn and broken free
Never notice the nightstand music
Everything outside is on fire or frozen stiff
A moan to break the snow

LITTLE BONES

I hate your hair in my mouth. I miss your hair in my mouth.
Full blast is your lighthouse voice box. You are a solution to
the meandering story.
The outboard engines of madness throttle. My ships seize.
But there you are, skating upon the freezing surf. Summoning
new seasons.
Summer concedes to your eyes.
Welcoming me, a kind home.

DEEP COVER

BEST THING SHE SAID WHEN WE MET
You dress like a narc.

WORST THING SHE SAID AFTER SEX
I hope we're okay.

BEST THING SHE SAID AFTER SEX
I don't want to even be on this planet anymore.

WORST THING I SAID AFTER SEX
Do you happen to appreciate close-up magic?

BEST THING SHE SAID TO MAKE ME FALL IN LOVE
AFTER MONTHS OF SEX
It was so good, you almost knocked out my mouth guard.

BEST THING I SAID AS HER FACE TURNED TO
SORROW WHILE SHE OFFERED ME MUSHROOMS
You are actually under arrest.

THE AWFUL SOUND OF PACKING TAPE

Boxes being built are a terrible sound— a brown, temporary sad.
She bought a lot of small boxes. I wonder if she is moving into a place with stairs,
but I don't get to know anything anymore.
The men humming at her new place begin pulling up in their horndog motorcade.
She is unpacked, without electricity, and she is free.

I hear the 4am housewarming parties starting across town.
The skinny musicians line up and sing into her mouth. So many small boxes.
Boys, if anyone spots my snowplow keys in there,
a gold tooth with a moon etched on it, or something I said in
an everlasting tone,
please ring me at the abandoned luncheonette of roaming men.
719-266-2837

HELLO. IT DOESN'T MATTER.

In my handsome garden I look down from the heavens
and you two are beautiful together and it doesn't matter
and you look at her and see that she's your only truth
the wood-splitter of your heart and it doesn't matter
and he's your dream museum your favorite species marrow
sucking apprentice
and it doesn't matter and she loved you like a hidden God and it
doesn't matter
and he wants no one else but he sees it in her posture that she might
and it doesn't matter and there's someone better always and it
doesn't matter
and a bird crashes into his window he will wonder if the bird is lost
or if his window was in the way but it doesn't matter
and her hurt and hate for me is growing in her liver
and it's too large to cut out or she'll bleed to death and it doesn't matter
and he has a violence inside that lives in his sperm and I put it there
and it doesn't matter and she wishes she was designed better but
she wasn't
and it doesn't matter and you want her to look up and love you again
to love you harder than sneezing with your eyes wide open and it
doesn't matter
and he will wish his season wasn't all over so soon but it is
and it doesn't matter and you'll both wonder why did I make your
ending so grueling
and you will hunger to know but I won't answer and it doesn't matter

•

I love you, useless. Love is not the moon and sun swapping space.
It is one eating the weaker nightly. One of you will win.
So just drink your wine and cry and become a flood.
Drink down all that loneliness.
Sometimes it will feel like it's just you and me in the garden,
but sometimes, it's really just you.

You thought you two were a church that couldn't be torn down,
a synagogue that couldn't be unbelieved in.
You'll think, wasn't I designed for her? Why must we stray?
You will look up and think:

Why don't you just un-design all this grief? Why won't you just make it go away?
Because it is in me and I need to be known.
I can't go away. I can never die.
Death and loss are my gifts.
If you know my pain, you can know my love.

I love you in rivers.

HOW THE BODY WORKS THE DARK

SUNLIGHT'S MOUTHPIECE HOLLERING

I serve the paths of your body and the tired
navigator of your heart. Rivers un-ice before us.
I'm not one season. I'm every season at once
and I hunger wail, storm-shutter clatter and caterwaul for your Spring.
We are a story of rivers, proud
and shoving wide the frosted mud banks,
breaking loose after winter,
pouring into another sea.

MORE

We kissed so hard
I could see how you were going to die.
We screwed so hot, lost and wild;
the rabbits outside felt their first-ever recorded dose
of Catholic shame.
We kissed, hollered and moaned such a song
that parrots and songbirds quit the crooning biz.
Failed at living alone. You can't masturbate with a hand full of feathers.
Let's go home and get gross.
You are a mansion dropped in a swamp;
we sweat everywhere and slide off everything solid.
Your long hair, black waterfalls freezing above
two clear pools.
I run my fingers over your teeth,
looking for metal, searching for losses.
I thrust too hard,
through the sheets, through your oncoming ghost,
past the mattress, onto the hardwood floor.
What am I doing down here?
What are all of these other men doing down here?
Hey. Hey. Soooo.
I get back into the sack and tiny-bite your collarbone,
a snap releases marrow, judgy parrots and daylight.
You command me to dine.
Two soft cinnamon soaked pear slices pressed together.
You arch—a bridge to luxuria.

Plumes of exhilarated sass streak over the sheets.
Tar pit eyes, your kiss
is thick.
Comforter rapture. Exhaust me like grammar.
Obscenity exciter.
I am a vigilante with a dumb pie-frosting gun. Balsamic seduction.
Snake coil rattle tongue symphony—song all over me.
Unison torque and lava wash.
Scream the roof off.
Pleasure bellow, hollow yellow. The sweet vowels you holler.
I can spell again.
Nipples reaching like smart kids,
your thighs muff-muff the world around me.
Cum all over my skull and squeeze like a tight migraine.

I enjoy your calls for God
because he should see how well we have finally learned
to undo his jealousy and sadness.
When I kiss into the apples of your shoulders,
you feel the pleasure
of all Gods
leaving us alone
in the garden
for good.
The morning of your thighs scarf around my face.
I drown, rise and become you, like cream in coffee.
In this rest, your limbs drape across me, holding a ragged shark diver's cage.
My secret licks the insides of your mouth. Safron in Applesauce.
I always
want the most lost version of you.

The lake looks like a limo window. I tongue the sunlight
on your back.
Rando Desire: an ache as great,
as crystal deep
as Crater Lake.
I fade
into a mouthful of hard light
stolen from the warm buffet line
of your spine.
Full.
You are screaming for the sap to crack from the foot of the Redwoods.
We fuck like everlasting August.
How you scream the American scream—
More. More. MORE.

DEAREST SOON

I think I may be in love with you, Soon.
Night breaker,
teeth like staring into the long bones of sunrise, sinister brunette.
Your leather, your soft pressure
set this weather off. Fifty-watt kiss.
How I am nourished by the night
chaos in your skin.
The service that overcomes me
when your legs ache.
I need you here simple. To reset the pulsing sea.
I want your breath of cinder flint, squalls of wonder.
How your body works the dark.
My love. My Soon. My sugarcoated
Carolina Reaper. My almost
death.

YOU MAY NOT MAKE IT OUT OF HERE OLD

They cried out for your sadness
like it was a celebrity.
Bring us more.
So you dug the mine deeper.
They told you your sorrow was
heroic, so you believed the awards.
I missed you
and shouldn't have told you.
Your closet, full of costumes.
Your belly, too full to fit laughter.
What's better than beauty
and sadness?
How scary that it almost made you happy
and you almost gave in.
You have read the same kind of book
over and over, grief zealot, reinforcing the easy theme.
You believe the news
that these are the most troubling times, your times,
but they're not.
They're just the most revealing.
Come back
and say everything like you know it's true
instead of the perfection
of wavering, quivering, nervous and wondering.

You may not make it out of here
old.

Geraniums
closing at night in unison.

MOP DUETS

Our Harley roars along the surf highway
and you are there,
curls of hair
thrashing in the salted daylight
on the iron getaway drug.
Your mall bra wanting
to burst into confetti and set the girls free.
Sun through our lips. Hands tight and fearless on my denim hips.
It is strange to know you are in a memory
while it's happening.
A roadside beer, a pop-top kiss so deep it comes again.
A hotel bed knocking on the walls,
looking for its lost children, sealed in the insulation.
You have lived so long in the deserted island of your job,
your eyelids the color of
bar light. The pre-shift mop dancing is such a loyal partner.
It's good.
The friends are good at this elevation. It's not the best.
Your hair—blue soon, then blonde, then brown,
then tomorrowland—
reveals how bad you want to change it all, but the money. . . .
A motorcycle buzzes by as you close it all down,
your hands gripping the mop handle.
Your pastel mouth, smiling a kind of safety,
a tired, night-shift love
that cannot be drowned out
by the aching, rumbling of pipes.

You are a complete
astonishment.

SUNDAY

Someday I'm gonna break your heart.
Sunday I'm gonna break your heart.
You will not want to know why.
You will only want me to know the pain.
I don't think I can.
I donated all my empathy to the 82nd Airborne.
I'll want you to know how it felt waiting for you to change
until I changed and could no longer serve you.
I pulled the trigger.
I'll find your face on a button one year later.
You as a fifth grader, longing
for friends in your huge glasses. God.
There it is.

DAMN THE GOWNS

Damn this face that looks like a gold brick dropped into oatmeal.
Damn the poet trying to turn my sorrow into a cool smell.
Damn the long gowns of those adored since high school.
Damn the gowns that fell swift for me.
Damn the ground I tilled for a month so you could have fresh
corn to remind you of your boring hometown.
Damn the twenty-two weeks I grieved losing you
and the forty poems that died on the couch.
Damn your new man and his cool vest and his skinny
skinny. Damn his hands in the persimmons.
Damn the memory of my
hands in the persimmons.
Damn how you asked me to not sing when
I cleaned the house.
Damn how you clenched your jaw when I asked
if you needed me.
Damn how I ate your disease.
Damn how I gulped
your pussy so I could be a brighter memory.
Damn the men honest as
Portland sunlight as they eat a bag of grapes
and tell you they're drunk.
Damn how hard it is to get the nerve
to put up Christmas lights these years.
Damn you for knowing what you want.

CRUEL MAGIC

Sad stories
are the best way to sweep the floor with your whole body,
head in hands, face to the floor, no God, no, no no.
I can't believe she is gone. I can't believe she is gone.

There is no return key for the landscape I miss.
There is no space bar that decreases the lean-away deadness of howling.

I will be alone tomorrow.
It feels exactly like (SCENE DELETED).
I was knee-deep in the stream for so long,
I thought we were the same force.
I forgot it could rise and wash me away. Spit.
I got carried until I was shallow in the mud.
Pressed face-first into the dam. Sad water.
Sad water don't ever make it to the sea.

The best song is always far from the hit.
She can love me weak from far away.
She could not love me over laundry, oil changes and weed whacking.
She missed being nude with me in a hotel challenging the sea.
It's not the real me. I'm often nothing nights.
I'm often nothing as night.

I don't trust anyone who tells it like it is when all we really do
is rework how it was. I can't believe she is gone.
I can see her collapsed on the kitchen floor
saying that this is her nightmare,
her hair sweeping from side to side, no, no, no.

I can't believe cow shit can become explosives.
I can't understand how images move through the air invisible.
I can't believe she is gone.

I want to watch bloopers on YouTube,
see someone else fall on their ass
and feel it shoot through my spine like an electric cable
spinning its way under the Atlantic. Me too.
I just want to be kissed tonight and not ask for it.
Can you see where I'm coming from?

I just want to be kissed tonight and not ask for it.
Can you see where I'm coming from?
It's way over there. It's a bad part of town and everything is changing.
Can I still see myself holding her dark hair
as she throws up the grief of knowing this is it?
The moment she took a break from the toilet
and let me have my turn to throw up five years of acid birds until she had to tap back in 'cause she had bigger birds to free?
Can I recall driving away from the sky we tried under?
Can I feel the collapse in my legs when I find
her tiny socks under the couch, reappearing like cruel magic?
Can I remember sleeping next to her,
exhausted on the couch and knowing that when I woke
it would all be over?
Finally waking, refusing to open my eyes for hours?
I missed the storms we played dead under in Texas.

I don't miss the breaking glass, the top of the lungs,
the bed under the couch of Texas.

The night - Bible black.

How cold can we get and forget we were inside each other's warm lives?

When the new wind comes it blows away the sun.
I used to pray for a flashlight that wouldn't die when I needed it the most. This dark is too long. Too wide.
I go to weddings and I cry, worried
that everyone
knows why.

MERCY SLEEPS

You are my midnight service.
Give me mercy sleep.
Then wake and weep out until you are distilled down
to just music and the gold blood I love.
You kiss me like Hell is real.
I rewrite all the days I spent without you.
I want four days at Avila Beach with you
until the breath-sucking sunset is finally made common
and we no longer devour each other's madness, we just
lay around, staring.

Brown eyes sliding away
into a soft
and loyal rest.

We will get coffee.

You won't expect it.

The stars aren't going anywhere.

I will fail at waiting to call you for a few days.
We will confess everything. It will feel so solid.
In fifteen months, I will never see you again.
The coffee will be remembered
and not much else.

PALACE OF SLOW DESCENT

I am with you in bed tonight,
in all beds, all nights.
Breaking into dream schools.
Freeing the nude classes.
Run for the cliffs. You can fly.
Dicks and breasts swinging
airborne, disassembling
the clouds. Every Pope's nightmare.
Wake up.
Geranium night paste over your eyelids
to soften the soft. Ginseng and tamarind
oil cover your back, quiet hands
glide around like abalone in low tide.
You feel good.
Grateful for you and all of our youth, escaped.
Glad you found me before the knives did.
My favorite era is still now.
Yesterday is a lonely place to vacation.
I want to die in your cheap bed, together.
It's gonna break any day now.
Kiss me until my head goes
all Scanners. Kiss me until I'm sick. Pearl diver bends.
Eve music takes the air.
The blaze cannot be unblazed.
What can be done
when even the fire engine is burning?
I volunteer to be taken by the sky. Nude.
Pissing on cemeteries. Arrogant in love,
slow and alive as the 405. Ribs rise, I feel
where they break. Simultaneous
overwhelming joy astronomy.
Your hair: dense foliage
under constellations—a purity of darkness.
Your kiss undeads me—
I smudge your gas station grapefruit ChapStick from your mouth
to mine and feel strong enough to begin
smashing upward
through the coffin's lid.

I LOVE YOU TOO MUCH TO DIE

You read my journal
which is fine,
but did you have to
proofread it?

THE FIREPLACE REACHES OUT TO ME

The fire in the fireplace looks like a wide-eyed Brahman bull
twisting for release from its tight cage.
I reach toward it, warming my hands, teasing the flame.
The pine cabin walls are terrified.
We are drunk and loading more logs into the bull's mouth.
Old age is upstairs so we sleep down here
and the minibar is here and it is full.
A bobcat knocks on the door
and politely asks for my trash.
I give him my dream journal.
He is so grateful.
A wall of books sits victorious and arrogant .
If I could just get to a place where I am left in a dusty cabin for decor.
She has passed out under an unspooky moon.
I love her.
She sleeps like an underpaid trucker.
I love her.
The clumsy pinecones plunk down on the tin, still fast asleep.
I love her.
The fire lurches toward her hair, it's fine.
I love her.
She is snoring and the trees are scared someone is sawing.
I love her.
The ashes of the fireplace ticker tape across the planks,
I motorcade wave that I love her.
The clouds of night keep blowing out the sky candles, I love her.
We are soft, forgotten things in the middle of nowhere. Her dad is
    gone. I am here now, eavesdropping on her dreams, a blanket
    clumsy over her legs. Can we live here? The fire is growing.
    In the dream, we meet. We're on an inner tube in the snow
    and everyone we love is alive. Her legs twitch, the beast in the
    fireplace settles down. She runs into a pageant of snowflakes; long
    white runways for winter's queen. She smiles into the couch, eyes
    closed, head warm in my arms.
I won.
We are made less terrible by each other.

Love Ends In A Tandem Kayak

END TIMES TIMELINE

It's the early 1970s.
I am born as a screaming kind of child. Oh God, Oh God.
Mom dips my pacifier in sherry.
I stop screaming. Wood paneling blurs.
I bliss out and forget the lonely rooms.

A preacher named Hal Lindsey publishes
The Late Great Planet Earth. It gathers the flock.
They swear the end is near and everything changes for us.

It's 1984 and Christ is coming to blow up the earth
as Madonna drops Like a Virgin.
I roll around in the dirt like she did at the MTV music awards.
I roll around alone singing out my need
to be touched for the very first time.

I am eleven years old and recognize that
it would be nice to fall in love before The Rapture.
To ascend hand in hand and not show up at the gates solo like a nerd.

The Rapture screams... Any day now.
I repent constantly because it could end tomorrow.
Sorry Lord, for burning Buzzy's arm while practicing our illusions.
Sorry for the obsession of flicking my nipples under the sheets.
Sorry for wanting this earth to last. Please let me rise with everyone.

Why care about anything else but heaven? This is all going away soon.
We sold so much stuff or gave it away. The things I loved.
I am a forced minimalist, a scared kid.
Scared of sleeping with the light off,
scared to not sleep on the floor,
scared of being left in Mexico again.
Scared of my friends pinning me down
and burning my hair again. Scared of someone taking
Woody Woodpecker.

The last year I'll feel comfortable talking to him
and having him teach me how to French kiss.
My parents watch 700 Club Christian News, and
the Trinity Broadcast network a lot. Lindsey is on all the time.

The Book of Revelation and its love of the coming apocalypse
gets real popular. Antichrist obsession rises. We will elevator to
heaven soon. We will rise into the friggin' air!
I learn to jump my bike off a curb by myself.

Lindsey makes links between the Bible, modern materialism,
the distant Cold War, gas shortages, and Satanic rock and roll.
I have my own problems, I got a crush on Alyssa Milano.
She is far, and it's all I want. I'll listen to whatever she likes.
I hope it's "Crazy for You."

Every believer in heaven forgets that
living in a constant state of wanting,
of scared readiness and hopeful waiting, delirious pre-worrying
is hell.

Parents split. The pressure of too many un-truths.
They should have never married. Plates stacked too high.
It may be why I'm not married to this day.
Nothing in the future can be proven false, but an eleven-year old
could see it.

Magic fills a hole in us with either hope or deceit.
I am still waiting for a kind of believer.
Oh God, Oh God. My bed narrows each year.
Oh God, Oh God. I can't endure another bullshit meal of desire.
Oh God, Oh God. Don't let me get used to dining alone.

Every hairstyle at this party looks like the end of a rope.
I am still in the waiting rooms of love. I daydream. It is sherry.
The earth is reborn perfect. Clean people inhabit it.
Nothing is wrong. The weather is great.
The wind hollows out the canyon. There is no coupling.

One day, the inhabitants line up
to take turns walking off
a most beautiful cliff.

A WETSUIT TOO TIGHT

I remember my teen time as a wetsuit
I couldn't wait to peel out of. It never fit, and I looked bad in it.
Some kids fell under a spell of romance and lust early.
Seemed like everyone in love was a runaway.

I couldn't get anyone to take my virginity...
maybe because I played volleyball.
I also thought if I could ollie 180 on my skateboard
someone would find me very attractive.

Steve Martin on vinyl became my friend.
Styled by Emo Phillips and Harpo.
The pillow over my head was my friend when my parents
shattered nightly.

I have no lasting advice for you and your new world
except to tell you crumbs:
It all changes when you get a car and time.
It all changes when you realize love doesn't end in one person.

Your face just gets better and better. Not really.
Now can be awful, but nothing is as awful
as back then.

You'll learn that it's hard to hold your mom's scared hand.
It's hard for you to see her love for you is all of Appalachia.
It's hard to smile on when friends and fathers fade. Hard is good.

The best writers I know are lonely
and the best writers I know are trying not to be by writing.
Jot it all down sometimes,
and spend a lot of time farting around, not writing.

Chase stupidity and say, "We are having fun right now,"
when you're having fun.
Risk the platinum branding-irons
of heartbreak every time.

Learn the joy of some
and not all.
I have had some love. I have had some good times.
I have some friends and they have some love left for me.

Turn on your headlamp, roam, and illuminate
all that I missed.

QUIET AS A BURN PILE

Father, my blood share. The days are tightening.
I am quiet at your backyard trash burn pile.
We are waist-deep in your late seventies.

At lunch, I tell you, There's a crumb on your mouth, Pop.
You don't care and it's quietly funny to both.
Can you feel it?
Nope. It wants to be there.

I tell you I found a watch
in the pile—in the burning mound.
You stare down at the waiting dirt
and ask me if I said I had found a witch.

Yes, Pop. I found a witch and it has this melted
metal band. A little handcuff.
You don't flinch or laugh.

I tell you about your former love and wife, my soft mom.
That Ma's eyesight won't let her drive at night anymore.
That she is considering moving close to my sister's kids.
She is considering the end and how it will look to grocery shop,
having been gutted by God. And you don't
see the world beyond TV and AC and McDonald's.

I want to tell you
I used to hate you.
I used to want to beat you
harder than you beat me, I worked out to get strong,
to beat you
for your wander, misplaced anger, and belt buckle thrash.

But I just take another load of trash to the burn pile
and swallow my young hurt before making your potato salad.
You say, Thank you, son. You got it right. Pickles.
Yes, I remembered the kind with pickles.

I want to tell you how my life is crumbling,
as we stand over the garbage of your life, the waste in your wake...
I hear crackles of fire and grackles above, witch bone cinders,

you almost touch my hand.

Father. Endless Father. Cursed, Endless Father.
I plead my case for the last time.
Let me return this season to the silence we love.
To go back home
and wash down the burnt smoke of dying California
in a miracle of zinfandel and forget myself.

To walk across the sea to someone
who can't hold my want.
To sit alone like you, re-strategizing the past,
raising the dead like a grudge.

You are frail now.
You used to tell me to do as I was told
or you'd beat the "why?" out of me.
Pain taught me to do as I was told. Tell me what to do with my sad.

You and I used to wear a uniform,
and being ready to kill
meant you were a good boy who listened.
I was an obedient Pentecost.
Medals shining over my heart
for how hard I could obey—
a steady march to my honorable death.

I watch your toil and secret horror before me. In your I give up clothes.
You have a few years left, solo in the sticks.
Buying four foods. Potato salad. Chicken. Beans. Pie.
Tinker with the weed wacker. Leave it. You won't
let me fix the mower or take
out the trash or touch anything.

I need my things, you say. I wish I was a TV.
See me in your work, Father.
I watch you just to be with you,
as if some lesson can be learned.

This year, I am without a lover again, like you.
You want to end this way. I don't. I can't.

This next time I learn to love—
I will fall in love slower
and stay, like you once promised to Ma,
but every promise is a dish looking for a wall
in your trembling hand. I can't make out exactly what you mutter:

lowerme / medirt / lonermeformiles / boystuff /
toysinaburnpile / dicedpickles
/ turdofcow / cowardcufflinks / stinkofunused / usedupjunktrinkets/
mygoldmyallthatsleft / allmygoldjunk/ myburnmyburnmyburn

Teen me still see's you, steam coming from your mouth,
and I know the words I needed from you
froze in your throat. You clear
some crap from the garage and load it in the burn pile.
Wearing the slippers I gifted you. Ruining them.

Father. This terrible waiting.
I cannot ruin your last years
with the truth.

ACCIDENTAL SUICIDE

The house was drowning me.
My house was filled with love and linens.
A rainy world kept us indoors most of the time.

Our shoes next to each other by the door,
pine needles stuck to the wet edges.
A pie on the kitchen counter in a pink box
for dinner that night.

It can't officially be called our last pie
because it was thrown away three days later. After you tired.
Trash pie.
Thrown away when I moved out.

I didn't want to move out. I didn't want to feel ugly.
I didn't want it to end, even when I wasn't wanted.
I dream of drainage ditches filling.
I won't ever dream in this house again.

Photos in frames of places I can't ever go with anyone else.
It's like a dog pissed all over Spain and Vegas, Normandie,
Hat Yai, and Nangs.
Trash those too.

A tree in our yard fought the breeze that day, tapped the glass,
wanted to load its arms through the window
as the wind poltergeisted. O life in a hazard of rain.
O life somewhere else. O systems of surprise,
how you sneak up on me.

It was raining that morning, sad cartoon. Of course.
My house smelled like coconut cream. Once.
My house forgot how to summer.
My house forgot how to fuck.
My house forgot how to go easy on each other.

My house had a tool shed, and I cleaned it and never got a chance
to build anything.
It's all yours. It's your house. It's your dog now.

My home flooded in gray, and it fits you
like a catsuit, and I hope you know I don't own anything. Your body.
I wanted into your body. Dreamt, I finally got in like a shrunken
Dennis Quaid in Innerspace.

Inside I began to drown in all that water, and all I wanted was out
when I finally got in.

How do you not get drunk and call me slurring as a consolation prize?
First, you like being small in their veins, then you can't breathe when
the blood
thins, and you either die from smallness or get passed through
the intestines into
the light.

I have been shit out.
This house is flooding as I move my stuff into a U-Haul. I
accidentally said I never want to talk to you again.
I couldn't figure out the money. If I could've figured out the money,
I would have been a future most wanted. I could have looked like a home.
I know there is a home in me.

Empty as Dad's wallet. If I could have figured out the money,
I could have saved so much...
my uncle Gene's leg.

My dad said Gene committed accidental suicide. He wanted some
car insurance
money and tried to crash in a ditch, it snuck up on him fast—he braked,
but his bum leg must have freaked, accelerated too much, and flipped
the slight pickup,
and a married man drowned alone at night in Texas. I know how
badly he wanted
out, hand against the glass window, as if he was ever strong enough
to escape,
realizing his plan wasn't his plan, but someone else watching from
the treetops.

I can't die in the ditch.
I ordered coconut cake today at lunch. It had lemon in it,
and my eyes opened wide when I bit in
as if I had never had it before.

HUNGER SLING

In the dumbest year of the heaviest light
I worshipped nutmeg tea and staring.
I bowed down to television light.

I pressed my skin against the sunflower
wallpaper and prayed for arms to emerge.
The year of nothing is real anymore. Time erased. Saviors gone deaf.
The year of nothing is all I want to feel.

I was hungry at last.

The Danes call it hudsult or skin hunger.
The Dutch called it huidhonger, the want for contact.
I miss people I haven't met.
I love and long for people who once loved me—
the bad ones.

The French brought me confinema—
the jamming of confinement and cinema
when you are alone in a TV spree, becoming couchness.
I love the music of the Spanish potion: cuaranpena—
the marriage of quarantine
and sorrow.

★

Every hug, a noble risk.
I see them in the park.
I feel my skin nodding and reaching.

The following image will be
the next thing
you dream about.

Remove all the clothes from the closet and
lean into the coat hanger bones. What a crowd.
Paying someone to touch me and look under the hood
doesn't seem so kinky anymore—
it doesn't seem so scary to ask.

Every dog shall be hugged without request.
I've had some touch.
How the JoJo's burger girl's handful
of change felt like fresh
air without a mask.

*

I hold the pounds now.
I miss a theater of strange ones—I miss everyone's skin.
Shouting from a pulpit: I'm not good at this.

How long the year of dancing alone and steady sobbing.
Unbuckling your belt and crying at the mess,
maybe I'm being taught
how to remember what a Tic Tac is for.

My lonely dance reveals loaves of grief, a rusted
lust, an inherent magical sadness,
My beautiful, field-wide sadness.

Call all your friends, dying in the same way as you.
Thank your beloved pillow, the pretender, for being there.
Here's to making it this far
and toasting the chosen
who didn't sneak out from under the evil invisible
and had to soar early.

Here's to settling in the present couchness and being grateful,
soaked in orange turmeric stains,
learning to caress the walls and kiss the windows,
my heart and its ability to blank onstage,
my very real skin hunger rising,
begging this nutmeg tea
to taste like the chapstick of someone
born to come and save me.

IN SWEATS, IN DEATH

The sweatpants ended us.
Strange, you want to get closer to your lover,
and if you get too close for too long, you pass through them.

We stuffed the fuzzy cuffs of sex and desire
in a bag and threw it in the lake to rust—
the dead lake between us
somehow got deader.

At night, the hopeless bed reminds me
I used to be a person that was held.
Memory foam is the worst gift
for heartache.

I used to be soothed by light snoring.
I used to make the one with fangs laugh so hard,
her teeth would get snagged in the ceiling.

I used to love someone that would fuck me
with their eyes open
for two of the four years.
I felt her eyes turn away from me nightly
into some handsome world.

She said, "I'm just not attracted to you anymore,"
handed me a robe for the diving contest
into the ugly well.

I swam slowly in my happy fat, and now
I work out all the time,
hoping to fuck someone silly who has memorized
the way out, someone who doesn't like their cocktails sweet.
It's not working.

The pawnshop rejected the engagement ring,
said it was too unique—too hard
to melt down and find any value in.
So off into the Willamette you soar.

In the air, the ring sheds its memories
like cicada carcasses.
The cliffside proposal, the Sunday roast, the first time on skis—
they floated there in a pink mist
as the ring slipped
from its skin,
plunked—
O
O
O

and then those white gold, tiny diamond
and Honduran wood memories
wheezed into nothing.

In my sweats, I bake sweet potatoes
until they are black
and sweet enough
for me.

CROOKED CONSTELLATIONS

I am quiet in the insomnia apartment.
I feel a lead hand shove my chest,
reduce me down to the kitchen floor.

Too many of my single friends my age
died of heart failure, last short breaths on the floor—
last thing seen, crumbs—
and they didn't have weak hearts,
they had big hearts—too big
and they didn't have the money to fix it
and burst from empathy and want.

All the constellations
are her crooked body sleeping
when I am alone.
Something was mounted to her.
I couldn't unsaddle it.

The world isn't set up to be single.
I didn't want to be single.
I see the mirror disassembling me.
I look like someone who will start the diet
tomorrow
again.

I stay in it longer than I should.
I am waterlogged and pruney
near the end. Loved 'forever' too much.

Forever is an orphan:
a word you once were excited to adopt,
but because of its boorish behavior,
it is a word you no longer wish
or need to see
or owe anything to at all.

When I look
at the car we bought with the bad emergency brake,
it is so sad.
It is too big of a car

and begs me
to sell it to a family, clumsy with the Cheerios.

I am alone, and you are in love again
and there is no more talk of fairness,
and I have burned through so much
mouthwash trying to relearn
the human trash heap of online dating.

No one has time for a new story.
Two a.m. is too cold to smile,
too quiet to unbrass the dawn with singing,
so it sounds like someone is with you.

Don't wear these clothes to bed again.
Go stretch.
Go eat.
Remember you are bad at stocking the fridge.
The grocery is open late. Would be good to see a person.

At Perfect Foods Market
there is a howl in the meat department, "Make it quick, Steve!"
and a sign above says fresher than fresh. All willing meat.
Carton of eggs! Sale! One dollar!
What a deal.

Someone has partitioned them into 2 per little carton, for that single life!
Three-month supply of toilet paper!
It's just two rolls.
Oh.

Everything is slimming down around me.
The big box store was busier. "I want to sample and frump!"
Families buy in bulk and frump cozy all day.
The dessert section here is empty.
The tissue section is empty.
The wine aisle is empty.
The diaper aisle is stocked full.
The flower department is bored.

The words family-size have been censored from every package.
The lights inside are dim.

The floors are slippery.
No flirting after one p.m.

Of course
it's always been emotional
self-checkout.

It feels like an art installation,
the wall of alcohol, little airline bottles,
buy one, get five hundred free and build
some sort of fortress for dum-dums.

I am home.
I am keeping some dumplings in the bag.
Being single is leftovers, is a memory of a good meal and enduring
it again.

I always just want one glass of wine,
but it always tastes like shit a day or two later
and corking it feels like I gave up,
so I just drink it all.

Tonight I'll eat all the dumplings.
So I don't have to see them again.
I am so sick
of reliving everything.

MURDER OF THE MIDNIGHT JEWELER

When I am in love
I try and make the stars
more than they need to be.

I try to say they are
the work
of some loving midnight jeweler.
Drilling, welding, and setting stones
in the long, glooming, achromatic bands above.

And it's a bit much.
I am tired of miracling everything.
It's a fridge, not a glacial coffin of nutrients.
They're stars. Not a glitter implosion of wonder.
They don't care. God has a kink in her neck
and can't look down anymore.

Why should I keep looking up for answers?
When I am lonely, there are fewer stars
and less sidewalk whistling,
and I hear the plants screaming for daylight
and the birds begging for help
instead of songing.

I don't belong in the logical world.
I want to be the midnight jeweler again.

But it seems like the moon just orbits and orbits around the earth
and can't just move on. Is it a sign of longing?
What if it's a tipsy moon each night,
intently listening, windows open
as the humming earth does the dishes?

Like the moon, I have a job to do—
to magnet around love like a compass needle, yearning, wanting,
lusty as a boy with a cantaloupe warmed in the microwave.

I want to be the midnight jeweler again.

Where my job is to make out in under-heated hot tubs,

to get hexed by wealthy warlocks and gun nuts,
to have shitty writers want to kill me,
and to have lovers draw my shape in the sand until
the tide comes to do what it does best to the shore.

Before the murder of the midnight jeweler,
I was
animated dust.
A chatterbox to strangers.
A force that renamed things.

I saw things no one saw.
I was a full magic trunk.
An odd camera.
The mood ring of Athena and Lenny Bruce.

When I am lonely, the supernatural
is just natural.
When I am lonely,
my phone is pretend-broken, just an ear warmer.
A scrollable photo album of half-truths.

When I am lonely, I don't remember
what I have.
I keep orbiting around the last good thing.
All my assets turn invisible in lonely light.

I need to be burnt and freed into the air
like a paper lantern, released with the best of intentions
of releasing a wish
but remembered for catching a breeze, igniting the bag,
falling fast, streaking the black sky in fire,
scorching a little league field
as a cold wash of stars
hovers blindly above.

WEIGHTED BLANKET

Most people don't tell their kids
that much of life is goodnight dreams.
Goodnight, far away friends.
Goodnight, former soft ones.

We don't reveal to kids how some danger is fun
and whiskey hurts, and you need it to hurt,
and loneliness makes you stupid.
Goodnight, good choices.

We have a hard time telling kids
the wheels slip off. For every kiss
remembered, there are a dozen pictures of lovers
tossed in the burn pile. You wish them well.
Goodnight, ninety-nine-cent romance novels.

We wish we knew more truths earlier to ease this life.
We aren't trained how to fight right
without swinging wild and breaking our own jaws.
Goodnight to hopes of leaving
this world scarless.

We settle into the weighted blankets of night.
We aren't sure how to handle it
when the love of your life shows up, a suffering comrade
sitting across from you, agreeing that dry crepes
are the end of our species.

We aren't sure how to imagine the future
the first night you smell her brain, her beautiful circuitry
audacious in front of you, ready to destroy the love you knew,
smelling like a night sky full of Hawaiian pikake, and you are buzzed on
    it.
Goodnight solo laundry day.

It's nice to be haunted.
When she is gone, she is still there.
You begin to learn the codes in each other's little lighthouses,
she falls for your caramel fading twang.

You fall for her gentle want at the bar,
a queen hiding her crown under miles of curls,
still bouncing in the dim light of Ye Rustic Inn,
still not knowing it's a date until you offer to pay,
wing sauce on your Kenny Rogers Roasters face.

You're done. She holds you. You're done.
Now, there's music when there's no music.
In the dawn, a song to sing to the kids, a new warning:

Good morning my stumbling and bruised ice skate denier.
No one knows how to do this! Many know how to do this!
Good morning my inferno carousel.
Good morning my pile of Peeps destroyed in the microwave when we were high.

Good morning my tennis swing screamer.
Good morning my High Plains snow light.
Good morning my low tide, swamped-up porch song.
Good morning my shower jukebox and bad joke librarian.
Good morning my positivity forklift, lifting me from a sea
of boundless anxiety
into the rickety porno treehouse fortress
of your crumbling body.

Good morning.
The world is fading around us.
Good morning anyways, endlessy, my dear.
You will live in me, unburied.
Good morning, again and again,
until the wheels fall off.

SMALL WINDOWS IN THE YOGA PANTS

I wish it was Crème Brûlée Monday or Smash in Public Day,
but it's Laundry Day on the road again.
The clock ticks
like it's trying to get a hair off its tongue.

I'm on a big fat Yamaha Super Ténéré 1200 motorcycle
talking into a little helmet microphone, yelling
back at the wind in my ears and the ceremony before me
of a road unwinding like a celluloid film reel.

It's wonderful air to haul ass in, and I'm
trying to record this feeling as it happens.
Harry Nilsson at the bottom of my lungs,
commercial jingles for grocery outlet,
the subconscious unraveling along the tarmac.

Don't think of what you miss.
Record how beautiful a life with no appointments is.
I am quiet for days, except when screaming into the recorder.
Screaming close to death at 85 mph along the Beartooth Highway.

It's Fall in Lust Friday! Nope. It's just Laundry Day. Settle down.
I put four quarters in the wall machine for fabric softener sheets.
The older woman smiles at me, folding with sensual deliberation.
In the other aisle, a woman runs her nails across her long legs, lazily
fingering her phone, exhaling tiny and scrolling.

What's everyone eating in this town? Sex ham?

I was about to tell you how Bozeman, Montana,
feels like a horny Christian yoga retreat.
Two yoga moms sit down next to me at
the Farmer's Daughters breakfast cafe.

They just got done working out
and they smell like orchid Bounce dryer sheets. Little sheer windows
into their athleisure, diamond shapes up their thighs.
I listen. I listen and sip.

They ask about my jacket, nervous that I am dirty and
don't want to be bothered.
It feels so good to speak to someone.
It's Kevlar. Its an armored jacket, in case I fall.
"Well, don't do that."
It's all I try to do.

It would sound like poetry, if it wasn't surrounded by nervous giggles.
I ask them about their day. They skip it.
"Your bike is beautiful."

I want to say, you're beautiful. And
your husband's a liar. Get your hair knotted and your neck sucked.
Who wants to get on the back and smell their way back to life
and ruin their marriage?
I have room for one.

We can get you some warm clothes at Cracker Barrel.
And the good hashbrowns.
I want your yoga tights against me. I like the windows into your skin.
I want to hug you goodbye at the airport and not say anything,
your fake duck lips double pouting to kiss me one last time.

But it will never be as good as our kiss
by the bison field near the Chief Joseph Highway
where the twelve-point elk came
and stared at you getting it from behind.

Thanks. I like the blue rims.
Those are nice rims you got. Wish we could go for a ride.
One at a time ladies. Have a good weekend.
You too.

Off I ride into the skyline of fleece and guns,
puffy vests and raised trucks,
abortion billboards and Skechers everything,
a Costco country I am learning to love
as steady as the engine noise between my legs,
and I keep trying to sing with my visor open
without eating a bumble bee, wondering what dirty ass
muse sent me the phrase Sex Ham
when I wasn't ready for it.

BREEZE ADMISSION

I am afraid there is no one left.
I am afraid that what I had was as good as it gets.
I am afraid no one will want me that way again.
I am afraid I'll be haunted by her perfect orgasm cosmology.

I'm afraid she doesn't miss my cock or oaky kiss or hazel-hazel.
I'm afraid I'll never taste her body again, the deep broth
and chipped citrus.
I'm afraid I will never want to stop sucking all her down feathers
into the blankets of my body.

I am afraid she got bored,
no,
that I expired.
I am afraid she'll get excited about the newness
of stronger hands and cool city smilers.

I am afraid she won't dream about the adventures we planned
as hard as I still do.
I am afraid there's not enough in here.
I am afraid that I will see her tangy smile when declaring devotion to
a new
medicine cabinet.

I am afraid I still want to record her sound,
hands across skin sound,
her suffering dead moan sound,
when I rub her shoulders deep sea sound.

I am afraid no one will want my outdated song.
I am afraid that it feels normal without me,
too fast, too easy to shed.

This is how living is for a body covered in antennaes.
I am learning to reconcile the fact
that it isn't hard for anyone to be without me.

Why did I agree to meet?

I am afraid she can tell I jerked off to a video
of her laughing, about an hour before we have coffee to talk about
how great we both are doing.

I'm afraid I'll go back to praying as the loneliness gets so bright.
I'm afraid I'm looking for something invisible to lean on
which always gives way.

I am tired of looking for a love that is the full force of the hurricane.
Some people live good with just a little breeze
to keep them cool in the heat.
They seem at ease, fearless,
like the love they have is easy as looking at a mountain
without having to climb it
to enjoy it.

THE FIRST KISS AS THE LAST KISS

The first kiss was heavy-heavy
and the last kiss was murder.
The last kiss was too much teeth
and wondering when to run
to the deep snow and dive
to cool the heat.

The last kiss, it ended me
and the last kiss was hunger
for another last kiss
that was less of a gold hardening in the throat
and less wanting air
and new jewelry.

The last kiss was known to be
the last kiss by the other party.
The last kiss was brutal and soft
like the slobber of shore break.
The last kiss is always on a couch
you can never lay on again.

PHLOX

The summer of wallow too hard.
The summer of finched color.
Sidewalk drunks assassinated my birds
of paradise. We could still be together.

I deserve every morsel of paranoia.
The night is still hunting me.
Does this jacket make me look like an exit?
We could still have the child.

You summoned me
like I could skip the line at the fair
for watermelon summer.
We could be one admission apart.

You reached into the rind with a lead fist
and pulled out the center,
and my heart stopped.
We could have better lives.

You crammed it in my mouth, and my heart
beat again. Magical animal.
We could resurrect the sails of desire.

Pulp gulp. Grandeur
dripping down my face like a teen pink sunset.
Your godless face, your gift to my puzzle.
We could be in pillows.

My tears flow
for some dog
to come and taste.
We could try and try after trying.

You forgive me, and Death Valley
is blown from every map.
We could wander and end.

You forgave me.

Arms full of phlox,
and I vomited monarchs.
We both hear children scream in the park,
not sure if it's joy.

We could be us
if surrender
was on the table.

I ALSO HATE SEEING A BABY IN A LEATHER MINI SKIRT

Big Sur steams.
Plaskett Beach is a weird place to be alone
because it's so pretty
and there's no one to tell.

I ride the licorice curves.
Kids climb dead trees.
Turkey vultures hulk over the flattened skunk.
Light a fire.
Think of the time when I traded love for peace.

Justin Townes Earle is singing for Memphis mornings
into the camplight
and I am a kind of silence
and silences are broken
and a southern heart is heavy
and everyone can see me blown apart.

One beer exploded the good one,
down to one cheapo left.
I don't want to drown in any river,
don't even want to know why it sounds
so romantic to me this year.

Sit in the warm sand
singing don't give up please don't give up
at the top of my lungs.
The gulls are scared of me and should be.
I am bloated on the serene.

Time to start the new year's list of awful feelings
and
figure out where I can burn it.
The night is a train that breaks down.
The night is a skeleton wishing for the skin of daylight.
The night is a baby with a sparkler in a leather skirt.

I am cold under my clothes
under the embering light of morning
wishing there were lips to kiss

or hot dogs.

I have this morning forever now as
the music of dead men
call from the speakers
reminding you
to respect
where you're at.
It's fine that it hurts
at least I can feel another ocean
than the one I lost
for a little while.

A MERCY MOST NATURAL

The desert apologizes for all the killing.
There's little comfort, little mercy in the wilderness.
Mercy is not natural.

Stop under
an overpass
as it rains.
The air is clean as warm sheets until
the high desert rains come and tease the dying
Badlands with creosote and thin mud, ground steaming.

I step into the rain.
A momentary break
from the suffering light above.
I walk into the applause of tiny drops in puddles as the storm dies.

Damp air of sage blooms,
broadcasted tumbleweed.
I go from soaked
to bone-cinnamon dry
in minutes.

I assign myself to this world.
I need to stay.
I forget why I need to stay.

All my sorrow a desert,
all the campsites I can afford, booked.
I put a Motel on a credit card and cry.
Pepsi and Funyuns.
I hate Pepsi.
I hate not having money.

I don't cry, I soft rain. I rain often,
common as a night stroll in the groomed burbs.
I rain to scare the desert inside, to hold it from expanding.

I'm dying in a nation of broken trampolines.
Knowing where you are is different
than knowing where you're supposed to be.

I feel it all when I am alone in a motel.
Polyester comforter air.
Blacklight nightmare.

Writing all this feels like I am wrapping a coat tie around my neck,
fastening it to the doorknob
and wondering if I'll cum or suffocate.

I wish someone was here to annoy me.
I wish someone would steal the comforter.
I wish my bed vibrated.

On a family trip, I'm so small. My parents got an earthquake bed
at a motel 6 and you put eight quarters in
and the headboard was mounted to the wall,
so we couldn't get to the plug to turn it off.
It shook all night long like the world's
saddest AC/DC ballad.
My mother slept next to me on the floor. That was so good.

Dry lightning is an eerie thing falling from heaven. Sudden thud.
When I want a traffic light to change I say ". . . aaaaand now!"
Pretending I can call the flash down, I yell "aaaaand, now!"
Timed it right once and killed
a shy lobby of groomsmen.

Love is too short for shy.
It appears my job is dreaming
of you, and I have been drinking
on the job.

I was mad.
I stayed—
I am the one who stayed. No one else to be mad at.

I smell the soft bonfire chemicals
of someone smoking in the parking lot.
My father's brand.
I lean on the rail. A voice from below says, "Hey, can I come up?"/
"Who are you?" I say. /
"An anvil. An anchor. A fridge full of foods that will make
you unfuckable." /

"Come on up."

Maybe I won't be in this hotel, on this road long.
Maybe I will sprain my ankles, whiskey tango solo on rotted dance floors
and enjoy my last alone.

When you tango alone,
you look like an idiot.
You look like a widow without a shadow.
You look like you can't let go
of a prom ghost who is politely passing the time with you
while waiting for their lover to come back from the bathroom.

I try but can't let go of a hope that I will find a prom crasher,
a flamenco turmoil, a tempest of storm-twisted flowers
who whispers in my ear, boy, boy full of useless rain.

I have come
to erase your grave.

VISION BOARD

I have something scary to tell you:
In Mt. Carroll, Illinois,
Jim and his wife set up the Raven's Grin Inn,
a five-story former hotel that since the '80s has been converted
into a come-when-you-want haunted house.
They live in it.

If Jim is in a good mood,
the tour can last three hours.
There is a cat named Mr. Tuxedo,
a six-foot skull mounted to the house,
slides that vanish down into secret passageways
and a New York taxicab mounted like it crashed into the front door
permanently.

You can rent the whole thing and play hide-and-seek.
They love each other.

I don't want to die in an office.
I want to find someone who yells Bingo
when they bust.

Take me to a weird beach in San Pedro and sleep on me warming.
A love life that is one long courtesy flush.
A partner who never asks which Aloha I mean.
Goof-whistler in the garden of serious men.

Take me to a hot spring and ruin me. Boil my sorrow
and rust me out
with your half-smile.

Fill the watermelon with vodka and take it
to the party and don't tell anyone. Not even the kids.
Throw their iPads in the fire and say it's a sacrifice to the digital gods.

Microdose with me under the Christmas lights.
I want days with you that are easier than pancakes.

Friendlier than a Canadian who grew tired
of being labeled as just friendly but

then went through a really hard time and leaned on their friends
and made a conscious choice to take a poll and the winning vote was
to get hella friendly again.

Pornstar courage in your heart. Bingo!
I'm trying to love you.
I'm a trying person.
I'm trying like a melody
that needs to be remembered.

I'll be a good business.
I'd love some company.
I want to build something
very, very
scary with you.

IT'S ALL COMEDY

Never watch the Glen Campbell documentary
I'll Be Me
when you are alone.

The film where Glen slowly forgets
all his songs, forgets who loves him, helpless
as a waterfall, and dies
wondering what people are.
The world is all strangers.
Why does anyone like this?

You
will cry
the Pacific.
You will wonder
why you watched that
and not Hot Rod.

Can't sleep. The night
holstered
by the dawn.
Who loves me?
Who loves me beyond my use?
Who loves me when I am assless
chaps at the funeral?

Frantically write down the names
of the ones who truly love you. C'mon.
Don't you wish you could fill the page?
Cry the Atlantic.

You get
what you get.
I wish I didn't know
it's all comedy.

The marionette has stumbled forward, revealing
the strings beginning to fray.
The soil beneath the stage, the hungry mouths of the dead
unglued and wide open.

Love isn't someone.
Love is a little moment.
Love is a coat that fits.

To try love on is to smile back at death,
to welcome stars as holy teeth
in the blueberry-stained mouth of night.

You will recall the pine and citrus synthetics in the shampoo smell.
Recall your hands in the wet hair of your slow exit,
when she could still look you in the eyes while inside her.

Recall the swim in the Long Beach lagoon
and how the water tasted like corn tortillas
which is not good, but you were warm and stayed in.

Recall when the searchlights of morning shined through my window
and you woke slow and I made you tea and you thanked me
and introduced yourself like it was day one. Hello, dummy.
Hello, dummy.

Recall your Mother not lonely in her mind, in the endless garden.
Recall how the Sandy River water was mint
and Coors Light-cold and how the reborn forest smelled
like smoked cotton candy.

Recall the dog you adopted together
and how it was scared of the sea, the day it bolted
into the water for its first swim, confused,
scared, and then happy it got the ball. Me too. Your dog now. Cry.

Recall when you didn't live in a city
that made you weep
in the long goth gray.

Recall what sunlight fixes
until it is gone. Did I already write that?
Recall the war to remember how wanted you felt in sunlight.
Recall miles of briar and the sour blackberries among the sweet on
your fingers.
Recall how the flavor that would come back when you washed the stain.

Recall the lean months
without meat or good fruit.
Recall and welcome it all.

Nothing can fuck me until
I spread. Love. Come again and fuck me up.
I remember. I'm okay with another stumble.
I remember how to get up and do shit.
I remember it all.

This
is the way
I fight
God.

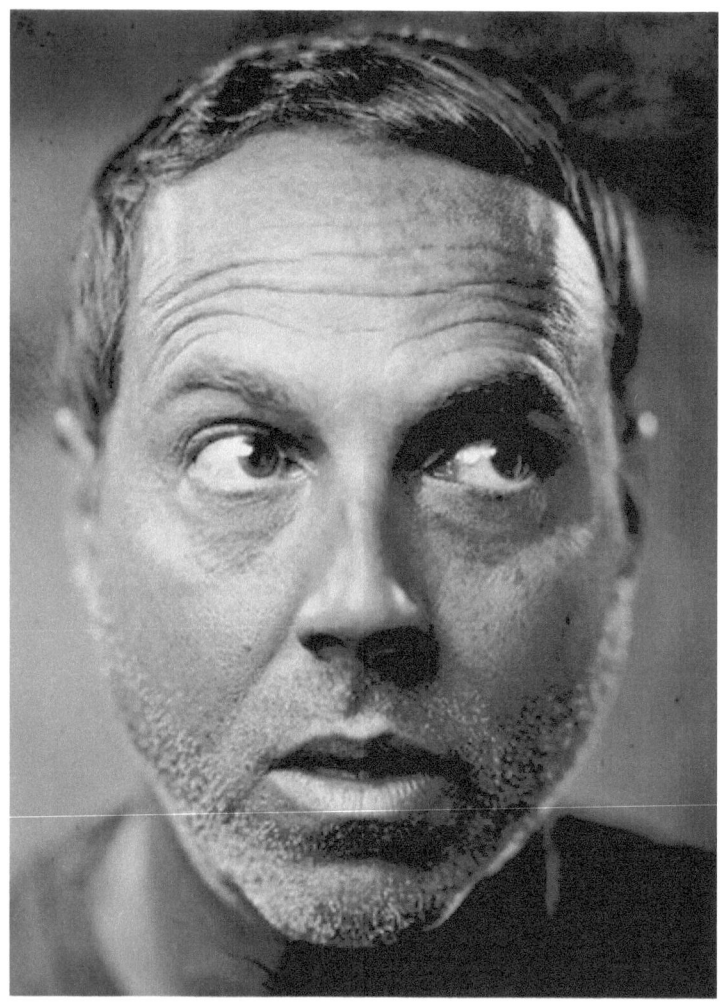

About the Author

Derrick C. Brown is a Storyteller & Writer | Comic | Award-winning poet | President of Write Bloody Publishing whose innovative blend of poetry and comedy earned him Paste Magazine's Comedy Album of the Year in 2023. The New York Times celebrates his work as "a rekindling of faith in the weird, hilarious, shocking, beautiful power of words." He used to be a paratrooper for the 82nd Airborne, but finds writing to be harder. He is the 2025 poet laureate of Los Feliz, CA.

Brown often tours via motorcycle.

He is the author of ten books of poetry and four children's books, and winner of the Texas Book of the Year award for Poetry.

@derrickbrownpoetry

www.brownpoetry.com

Photo left, Noyel Gallimore.   Moto Photo by Matt Wignall

IF YOU LIKE DERRICK C. BROWN DERRICK LIKES...

all Write Bloody poetry books

Write Bloody Publishing publishes and promotes great books of poetry every year. We believe that poetry can change the world for the better. We are an independent press dedicated to quality literature and book design, with an office in Los Angeles, California.

We are grassroots, DIY, indie believers. Pull up a good book and join the family. Support independent authors, artists, and presses.

Want to know more about Write Bloody books, authors, and events? Join our mailing list at

www.writebloody.com

www.ingramcontent.com/pod-product-compliance
Lightning Source LLC
Chambersburg PA
CBHW032125160426
43197CB00008B/520